FOOD&WINE
BOOKS

FOOD & WINE COCKTAILS 2005

ON THE COVER Sumo in a Sidecar (left), P. 138
Gamma Ray, P. 139

AMERICAN EXPRESS PUBLISHING CORPORATION

ISBN 1-932624-02-3
ISSN 1554-4354

Published by American Express Publishing Corporation
1120 Avenue of the Americas, New York, NY 10036

Manufactured in the United States of America

FOOD & WINE MAGAZINE

Cocktails 2005

FOOD & WINE

AMERICAN EXPRESS PUBLISHING CORPORATION, NEW YORK

Contents

To create FOOD & WINE's first-ever cocktail book, we embarked on a major search for the country's coolest bars, restaurants and lounges and their best drink recipes. Our discoveries include the latest innovations from "bar chefs" as well as the finest versions of classics. (Recipes were perfected in our test kitchen—great fun while it lasted.) We also offer a cocktail clinic on mixology basics and a coast-to-coast nightlife guide. Please join us as we raise our highball and martini glasses to America's best cocktails.

EDITOR IN CHIEF
FOOD & WINE MAGAZINE

EDITOR
COCKTAILS 2005

COCKTAIL CLINIC

A few simple pieces of glassware that no home bar should be without.

HIGHBALL
A tall, narrow glass. Helps preserve the fizz in drinks served on ice and topped with soda or tonic water.

MARTINI
A long-stemmed glass with a cone-shaped bowl. For cocktails served straight up (chilled with ice, then strained). Oversized ones are visually striking but unwieldy.

RED WINE
A squat, balloon-shaped glass; stemless varieties are increasingly available. For fruity cocktails, punches and frozen drinks; a fine substitute for snifters.

ROCKS
A short, sturdy, wide-mouthed glass. For straight spirits and cocktails.

SNIFTER
A short-stemmed, wide-bowled glass designed to rest in the palm of your hand. For warm drinks and cocktails served on ice, as well as for spirits served neat (without ice).

WHITE WINE
A tall, narrow wine glass. For wine-based cocktails; a fine substitute for highball glasses.

FLUTE
A tall, slender glass. Helps keep sparkling-wine cocktails effervescent.

CORDIAL
A petite, tulip-shaped glass. For powerful drinks that are served in very small portions, dessert wines or liqueurs served neat.

PITCHER
A large glass container with a spout and handle. For big batches of stirred cocktails and punches; find one with a narrow spout that will strain ice.

MARGARITA
Similar to a martini glass, but with a curved bowl and wider mouth. For margaritas and frozen drinks.

HEATPROOF MUG
A durable cup or glass with a handle. For spiked coffee and other hot drinks.

PINT
A tall, slightly flared glass with a wide mouth and sturdy base. Possibly the most versatile bar glass. For stirring drinks, making a Boston shaker (P. 13) or serving oversized drinks.

Essential bar tools to keep on hand for making almost any cocktail.

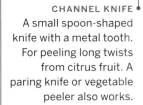

CHANNEL KNIFE
A small spoon-shaped knife with a metal tooth. For peeling long twists from citrus fruit. A paring knife or vegetable peeler also works.

WAITER'S CORKSCREW
A pocket knife–like utensil with a bottle opener. Preferred by most pros.

MUDDLER
A long wooden stick with a blunt end that's used to crush herbs, sugar cubes and fresh fruit. Look for a muddler long enough to reach the bottom of your cocktail shaker; alternatively, use a long-handled wooden spoon.

CITRUS JUICER
A shallow dish with a reaming cone, a strainer and a spout. For extracting citrus juice. Lemon and lime juices are best the day they're squeezed; orange and grapefruit juices can last 2 days in the refrigerator.

DOUBLE JIGGER
A two-sided device for quick, accurate measuring. Look for one with ½-ounce and 1-ounce cups. A shot glass with measurements works well, too.

COCKTAIL SHAKER

A metal or glass cylinder for mixing drinks with ice. The most common model is the **cobbler shaker** (left), which has a built-in strainer and a fitted top. The **Boston shaker** (right), the bartender's choice, consists of a pint glass and a metal shaker that covers it.

BAR SPOON

A long-handled metal spoon used to mix cocktails. Since stirring doesn't cloud a drink with air bubbles, it's preferable for cocktails made with spirits only, such as martinis and Manhattans, which look best served crystal clear. Also useful for measuring small amounts, or splashes, of liquid ingredients.

STRAINER

A round metal device used for straining mixed drinks into glasses. Pros favor the spoon-shaped **julep strainer** (left) for stirred drinks; it has fine holes for removing small pieces of ice. The **Hawthorne strainer** (right) has a semicircular spring that ensures a snug, spill-proof fit inside a shaker; also ideal for straining cocktails stirred in a pint glass.

Classic and innovative garnishes for all different kinds of drinks.

CITRUS WHEELS, WEDGES AND TWISTS
Wheels, or crosswise slices, of lemon, lime and orange are generally decorative; wedges can be used to add a squeeze of citrus to the drink. For long, narrow twists, use a channel knife (P. 12) to cut strips from thick-skinned fruit like navel oranges and jumbo lemons; use a paring knife or vegetable peeler to slice flat, thin twists.

EXOTIC FRUIT
Slices of five-pointed star fruit can adorn almost any tropical drink.

MARASCHINO CHERRIES
Developed in the early 1900s as an American alternative to pricey European cherries, almond-flavored (and artificially colored) red maraschinos garnish countless classics.

BRANDIED CHERRIES
Elegant, brandy-soaked morello cherries from France or Italy are available in specialty food stores.

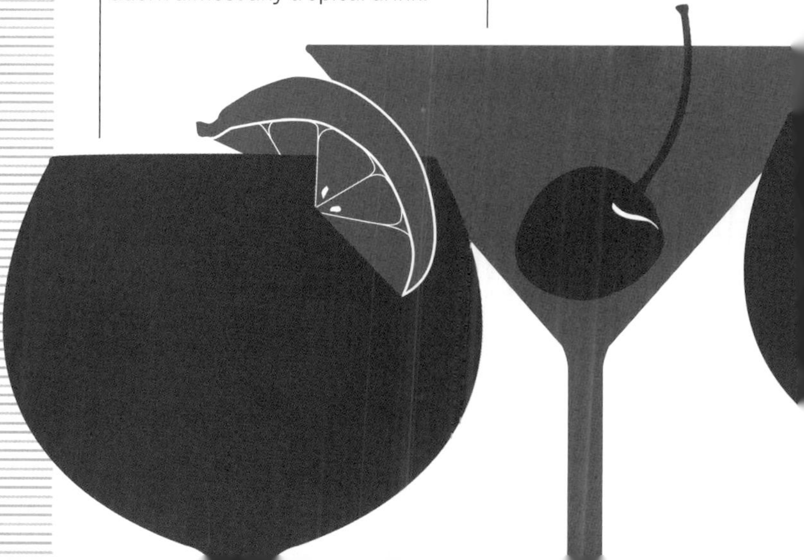

PINEAPPLE SPEARS
Great for tropical drinks, a pineapple spear looks best with the prickly rind intact.

LEMONGRASS SWIZZLES
Slice the root end off a 6-inch lemongrass stalk and peel off the stiff outer layers.

SUGAR AND SALT RIMS
A glass lightly coated with salt can balance the sweetness of a drink, while a sugar-coated rim can temper tartness (see P. 16 for how to rim a glass).

FLAVORED-POWDER RIMS
Mild powders such as Tang or cocoa work best for sweet or fruity drinks; rich or spicy cocktails can stand up to stronger ingredients such as chili powder.

GREEN OLIVES
Nowadays you can find cocktail olives stuffed with everything from tuna to garlic to habaneros. But for many cocktail professionals, a plain green olive such as the Spanish Queen remains the best match for a well-made martini.

VERMOUTH-SOAKED OLIVES
Many specialty food markets carry green olives steeped in dry vermouth—a perfect garnish if you prefer your martini very dry.

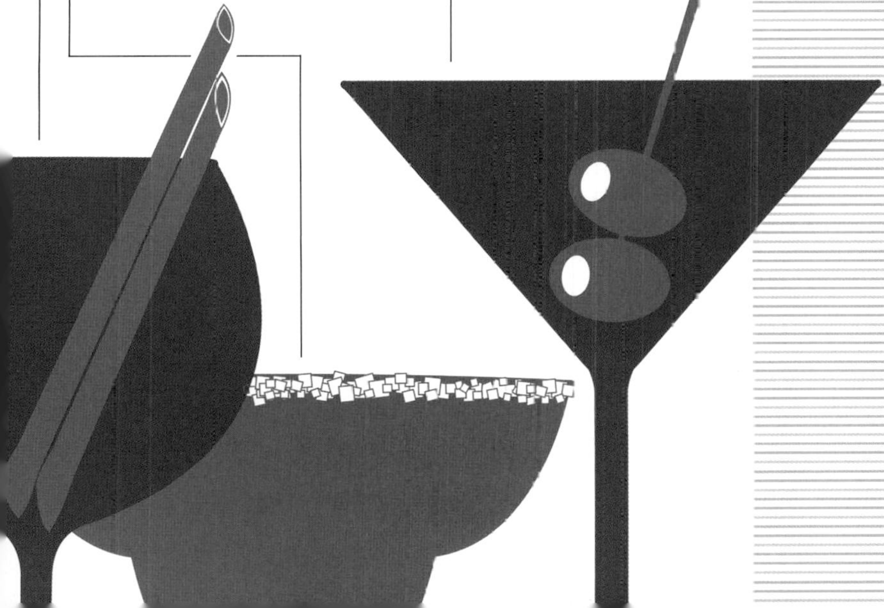

Everything you need to know to master a few fundamental techniques.

THREE COCKTAIL BASICS

CHILL A GLASS

Chilled glasses are essential for any cocktail that should be served cold. The easiest way to chill a glass is to store it in the freezer or refrigerator. If you can't spare the room, fill the glass with ice water and let it sit for several minutes. Drain the ice water before using the glass.

RIM A GLASS

To lightly coat the rim of a glass, place a few spoonfuls of salt (preferably kosher), sugar (preferably granulated) or other powdered or finely crushed ingredient on a small plate. Moisten the outer rim of the glass with a wedge of citrus fruit or water or a vibrantly colored liquid like pomegranate juice, then roll the glass on the plate, pressing gently, until the outer rim is lightly coated. Hold the glass upside down and tap the base to release any excess; don't let any fall in the glass.

FLAME A TWIST

Flaming a lemon or orange twist intensifies the essential citrus oils, providing extra aroma and flavor to a drink. Start by cutting a thin, oval, quarter-sized piece of zest with a bit of the white pith intact. Grasping the outer edges very gently between the thumb and index finger, hold the twist skin side down about 4 inches over a cocktail. Set a lit match an inch below the twist, then pinch the edges sharply together to propel the citrus oil through the flame and onto the drink.

SIMPLE SYRUP

This bar staple is one of the most universal mixers, essential to many well-balanced cocktails. Keep a jar handy in your refrigerator: it keeps for up to 1 month.

SIMPLE SYRUP RECIPE

Combine 1 cup of water and 1 cup of sugar in a small saucepan and bring to a boil over moderately high heat, stirring to dissolve the sugar, about 3 minutes. Remove from the heat, let cool and refrigerate in a tightly covered glass jar until ready to use. Makes about 1½ cups of syrup.

CONVERSION CHART

Most bartenders measure their drink ingredients in ounces. Here's a handy guide for equivalent tablespoon and cup measures.

OUNCES			TABLESPOONS/CUPS	
¼	ounce	=	1½	teaspoons
½	ounce	=	1	tablespoon
¾	ounce	=	1½	tablespoons
1	ounce	=	2	tablespoons
2	ounces	=	¼	cup
3	ounces	=	¼	cup + 2 tablespoons
4	ounces	=	½	cup
6	ounces	=	¾	cup
8	ounces	=	1	cup
16	ounces	=	2	cups
24	ounces	=	3	cups
32	ounces	=	1	quart

RED GRAPE & COCONUT REFRESHER, P. 24
Kittichai, New York City

CHAMPAGNE, SAKE & WINE

19

Lemon Sipper

In keeping with the restaurant's philosophy, the bar at Region emphasizes local ingredients. This drink uses mint from famed Chino Farm and lemons from nearby Cunningham Organic Farm.

Region • San Diego

3 lemon wheels
10 mint leaves
Ice
1½ ounces limoncello
2 to 3 ounces chilled prosecco

In a cocktail shaker, muddle the lemon wheels with the mint leaves. Add ice and the limoncello and shake well. Strain into an ice-filled highball glass and top with the prosecco.

Vanilla Pear Mimosa

In addition to great cocktails, Twenty Manning serves Black Angus burgers that are among the best in Philadelphia.

Twenty Manning • Philadelphia

¾ ounce vanilla vodka
1½ ounces pear nectar or juice
4 ounces chilled prosecco

Pour the vodka into a chilled flute. Top with the pear nectar, then the prosecco.

Clover Club Fizz

Very Venice Bar • Las Vegas

Noted mixologist Francesco Lafranconi puts an Italian spin on this pre-Prohibition cocktail by topping it with prosecco.

¼ cup raspberries
1½ teaspoons sugar
Ice
1½ ounces gin
¾ ounce fresh lemon juice
½ ounce peach schnapps
½ large pasteurized egg white (optional)
2 ounces chilled prosecco
Pinch of freshly grated lemon zest

In a cocktail shaker, muddle the raspberries with the sugar. Fill with ice, add the gin, lemon juice, schnapps and egg white, if using, and shake well. Add the prosecco, then strain into a chilled flute and garnish with the grated lemon zest.

Me & Mrs. Jones

Benjy's • Houston

Owner Benjy Levit named this drink after a 1972 Billy Paul hit, his wife's favorite song.

½ ounce sweet vermouth
½ ounce fresh lime juice
1½ teaspoons grenadine
½ teaspoon sugar
4½ ounces chilled Champagne

In a cocktail shaker, combine all of the ingredients except the Champagne and stir or shake briefly. Pour into a chilled flute and top with the Champagne.

SUDDEN HEADACHE
Elm Street Liquors, Chicago

Sudden Headache

ESL has two drink menus: one for such girly cocktails as Sudden Headache, served in Champagne flutes, and one for macho options like Arm Candy, served in pilsners.

Elm Street Liquors • Chicago

Ice
1½ ounces mango nectar or juice
1 ounce silver tequila
¾ ounce triple sec
¾ ounce fresh lime juice
½ ounce Simple Syrup (P. 17)
2½ ounces chilled demi-sec Champagne

Fill a cocktail shaker with ice. Add all of the ingredients except the Champagne and shake well. Strain into a chilled flute and top with the Champagne.

Bubbletini

A riff on the classic peach-and-Champagne Bellini, the slightly sweet Bubbletini complements the spicy food at this pan-Asian restaurant named for Tokyo's trendy nightclub district.

Roppongi • La Jolla, CA

Ice
1½ ounces vodka
1½ teaspoons peach schnapps
½ teaspoon Chambord
1½ teaspoons fresh lemon juice
2 to 3 ounces chilled Champagne
1 lemon twist

Fill a cocktail shaker with ice. Add the vodka, schnapps, Chambord and lemon juice and shake well. Strain into a chilled martini glass and top with the Champagne. Garnish with the lemon twist.

Red Grape & Coconut Refreshe

Top bar chef Albert Trummer, who makes many of his own mixers, is the cocktail consultant at this elegant Thai restaurant in SoHo.

Kittichai • New York City

- 12 seedless red grapes, plus 4 halved grapes
- 1 teaspoon dark brown sugar
- 2 ounces vodka, preferably Ciroc
- 2 ounces unsweetened coconut water
- Crushed ice
- 2 ounces chilled Champagne

In a cocktail shaker, muddle the 12 whole red grapes with the brown sugar. Add the vodka, coconut water and halved grapes. Stir and pour—don't strain—into a highball glass over crushed ice, then top with the Champagne.

Orange Twist

The poolside cocktail lounge of this restaurant-bar in Hotel ZaZa offers an expansive view of the Dallas skyline.

Dragonfly • Dallas

- Ice
- 1 ounce orange vodka
- ¾ ounce triple sec
- 1 ounce dry but fruity white wine, preferably Sauvignon Blanc
- 3 ounces chilled Champagne
- 1 orange twist

Fill a cocktail shaker with ice. Add the vodka, triple sec and white wine and shake well. Strain into a chilled flute, top with the Champagne and garnish with the twist.

Serendipity

Louis XIII • Edina, MN

Diners can request one of the plush tented "kissing booths" at this opulent Asian-inflected French restaurant in suburban Minneapolis.

6 mint leaves
½ ounce Calvados
Ice
½ ounce pear brandy
1 ounce apple juice
3 to 4 ounces chilled Champagne
1 thin slice of apple and 1 mint sprig

In a rocks glass, muddle the mint leaves with the Calvados. Add ice, the pear brandy and the apple juice, then top with the Champagne. Garnish with the apple slice and mint sprig.

Red Apple Bellini

The Social • Houston

This lounge's eclectic design includes pastel plastic sofas, a refurbished tavern bar from the South Side of Chicago and an enormous Absolut bottle covered with 1,000 coats of paint.

1 ounce sour apple liqueur
½ ounce chilled cranberry juice
3 to 4 ounces chilled Champagne

In a chilled flute, swirl together the sour apple liqueur and cranberry juice, then top with the chilled Champagne.

Paris Sunset

Many of the tapestries, antiques and African artworks at this restaurant, which is in a converted jewelry district warehouse, are for sale.

CAV • Providence

Ice
- 3/4 ounce Dubonnet Rouge
- 3 drops of Angostura bitters
- 1½ teaspoons sugar
- 3 ounces chilled Champagne

Fill a cocktail shaker with ice. Add the Dubonnet, bitters and sugar and shake well. Strain into a chilled flute and top with the Champagne.

Pimm's Imperial

Cocktail guru Tony Abou-Ganim revived this forgotten recipe, a version of a Pimm's Cup topped with Champagne.

Boa Steakhouse • Las Vegas

Ice
- 1½ ounces Pimm's No. 1 Cup
- 2 ounces fresh lemon juice
- 1 ounce Simple Syrup (P. 17)
- 2 ounces chilled Champagne
- 2 thin slices each of cucumber, apple and strawberry, plus 1 mint sprig

Fill a cocktail shaker with ice. Add the Pimm's, lemon juice and Simple Syrup and shake well. Strain into an ice-filled white wine glass and top with the Champagne. Garnish with the cucumber, apple and strawberry slices and the mint sprig.

Kir-tini

Diamond Head Grill • Honolulu

On Friday and Saturday nights, the W hotel's Diamond Head Grill transforms into the Wonder Lounge, a multi-bar club with DJs and dancing.

Ice
1¼ ounces Chardonnay
1½ teaspoons crème de cassis
1 to 2 ounces chilled Champagne
1 lemon twist

Fill two-thirds of a cocktail shaker with ice. Add the Chardonnay and cassis and shake well. Strain into a chilled martini glass, top with the Champagne and garnish with the lemon twist.

White Sanguine

Balthazar • New York City

A dry, unoaked white such as Sauvignon Blanc works best in this aperitif from Keith McNally's timeless SoHo brasserie.

Ice
1½ ounces white wine
½ ounce Chambord
½ ounce fresh orange juice
1½ teaspoons fresh lime juice
2 to 3 ounces chilled Champagne
1 orange twist

Fill a cocktail shaker with ice. Add the white wine, Chambord, orange juice and lime juice and shake well. Strain into an ice-filled white wine glass, top with the Champagne and garnish with the orange twist.

ASIAN PEAR MARTINI
Japonais, Chicago

Sakenade Ginger

Enormous hanging paper lanterns cast an atmospheric glow over this cavernous subterranean sushi restaurant in Chelsea's Maritime Hotel.

Matsuri • New York City

Ice
2 ounces dry sake
1 teaspoon finely grated, peeled ginger
1½ ounces fresh lemon juice
1½ ounces Simple Syrup (P. 17)
1 lemon wheel

Fill a cocktail shaker with ice. Add the sake, grated ginger, lemon juice and Simple Syrup and shake well. Strain into an ice-filled rocks glass and garnish with the lemon wheel.

Asian Pear Martini

The downstairs lounge at this restaurant on the Chicago River includes an outdoor space that's enclosed during the chillier months.

Japonais • Chicago

Ice
1½ ounces sake
1½ ounces pear brandy
1½ ounces pear nectar or juice
1 slice of Asian pear

Fill a cocktail shaker with ice. Add the sake, brandy and pear nectar and shake well. Strain into a chilled martini glass and garnish with the pear slice.

Kinkan

A balanced but potent cocktail made with orange vodka and muddled kumquats, Kinkan tastes best when shaken with an extremely dry sake.

Bar Masa • New York City

5 fresh kumquats
Ice
3 ounces orange vodka
1 ounce dry sake
½ ounce fresh grapefruit juice
½ ounce Simple Syrup (P. 17)
½ ounce cranberry juice
1½ teaspoons fresh lemon juice

In a cocktail shaker, muddle the kumquats. Add ice and the remaining ingredients, shake well and strain into a large chilled martini glass.

Green My Eyes

This sprawling, gallery-like space features work by emerging artists, graffiti on the brick wall and at least one DJ every night.

Levende Lounge • San Francisco

4 thin slices of cucumber
Ice
1½ ounces dry sake
1½ teaspoons Simple Syrup (P. 17)

In a cocktail shaker, muddle 3 of the cucumber slices. Fill with ice, add the sake and Simple Syrup and shake well. Strain into a chilled martini glass and garnish with the remaining cucumber slice.

Ichigo

Zengo • Denver

The cocktail menu at this restaurant offers both Latin- and Asian-inspired drinks, like Ichigo, which means "strawberry" in Japanese.

1 strawberry, plus 1 strawberry slice for garnish
½ teaspoon sugar
Ice
2½ to 3 ounces sake
1½ teaspoons peach schnapps
1 ounce guava nectar or juice

In a cocktail shaker, muddle the strawberry with the sugar. Add ice, the sake, schnapps and guava nectar and shake well. Strain into a chilled martini glass and garnish with the strawberry slice.

Napier

Tallula • San Francisco

This restaurant's name honors the eccentric actress Tallulah Bankhead; the cocktail was named for one of her many lovers, the British aristocrat Napier Alington.

1 ounce Fennel Syrup (below)
1 lemon wedge
Ice
1 ounce sake
1 ounce chilled club soda
1 lemon twist

In a cocktail shaker, muddle the Fennel Syrup with the lemon wedge. Add ice and the sake and shake well. Strain into an ice-filled rocks glass and top with the club soda. Garnish with the lemon twist.

FENNEL SYRUP In a bowl, cover 1½ tablespoons of crushed fennel seeds with 4 ounces of Simple Syrup (P. 17) and let steep for 2 hours. Strain and refrigerate for up to 5 days. Makes 4 ounces of syrup.

ICE WINE MARTINI
Blue Martini,
Birmingham, MI

Almond Martini

The Moroccan influences at this French-Mediterranean restaurant, whose name means "blessing" in Arabic, extend to this delicately almond-flavored martini.

Baraka • San Francisco

Splash of Lillet Blanc
Ice
3 ounces sake
¾ ounce almond syrup
1 toasted almond

Rinse a chilled martini glass with Lillet. Fill a cocktail shaker with ice. Add the sake and almond syrup and shake well. Strain into the martini glass and garnish with the almond.

Ice Wine Martini

A stage for live music replaces the typical backdrop of liquor bottles at this nightclub's main bar, which serves more than 25 signature martinis.

Blue Martini • Birmingham, MI

10 large seedless green grapes, plus 2 halved grapes for garnish
2 ounces ice wine
2 ounces vodka, preferably Ciroc
Ice

In a blender, puree the 10 whole grapes with the ice wine and vodka. Pour the puree through a tea strainer into an ice-filled cocktail shaker and shake well. Strain again into a large chilled martini glass and garnish with the grape halves.

BITTER QUEEN, P. 53
Martini Bar at the
Raleigh Hotel, Miami

VODKA

Cosmopolitan

The Odeon • New York City

The origins of the quintessential 1990s cocktail are not entirely clear, but many credit Toby Cecchini, a former bartender at this TriBeCa brasserie.

Ice
2½ ounces lemon vodka
1 ounce triple sec
1 ounce cranberry juice
1½ teaspoons fresh lime juice
1 lemon twist

Fill a cocktail shaker with ice. Add the vodka, triple sec and cranberry and lime juices and shake well. Strain into a chilled martini glass and garnish with the lemon twist.

Grappatini

Pazo • Baltimore

A dollop of whipped cream softens grappa's bite in this citrusy cocktail from Pazo, a Mediterranean lounge and restaurant in a historic 1880s boiler works.

Ice
2 ounces lemon vodka
1 ounce fresh lemon juice
½ ounce Simple Syrup (P. 17)
½ ounce grappa
½ ounce triple sec
1½ teaspoons fresh orange juice
1½ teaspoons fresh lime juice
1 tablespoon unsweetened whipped cream
1 lemon twist

Fill a cocktail shaker with ice. Add all of the ingredients except the whipped cream and lemon twist and shake vigorously. Strain into a chilled martini glass. Garnish with the whipped cream and lemon twist.

Lemon Drop

Turf Supper Club • San Diego

An aging collection of horse-racing paraphernalia adorns this 1950s-era restaurant, where you can cook your own steak and garlic bread on the dining room's self-service grill.

1 lemon wedge
Sugar
Ice
2 ounces lemon vodka
¾ ounce fresh lemon juice
½ ounce Simple Syrup (P. 17)
1 lemon twist

Moisten the outer rim of a martini glass with the lemon wedge and coat lightly with sugar. Fill a cocktail shaker with ice. Add the vodka, lemon juice and Simple Syrup and shake well. Strain into the martini glass and garnish with the twist.

Red Grape Sangria

Sushi Samba Rio • Chicago

This restaurant's new 2,700-square-foot rooftop lounge has a translucent fiberglass and steel roof that creates the feeling of outdoor space year-round.

6 seedless red grapes, plus 1 small bunch of red grapes for garnish
½ teaspoon sugar
Ice
2 ounces lemon vodka
1 ounce dry white wine
½ ounce lychee nectar or juice
1 ounce chilled club soda

In a cocktail shaker, muddle the 6 grapes with the sugar, then fill the shaker with ice. Add the vodka, wine and lychee nectar and shake well. Strain into an ice-filled highball glass and top with the club soda. Garnish with the bunch of grapes.

Lemongrass Lemonade

Fork • Philadelphia

This recipe makes enough lemongrass syrup for more than five drinks. For an easy and refreshing nonalcoholic cocktail, top an ounce or two of syrup with chilled club soda.

Ice
2½ ounces lemon vodka
1½ ounces Lemongrass Syrup (below)
1½ ounces fresh lemon juice
1 lemon twist

Fill a cocktail shaker with ice. Add the vodka, Lemongrass Syrup and lemon juice and shake well. Strain into a large chilled martini glass and garnish with the lemon twist.

LEMONGRASS SYRUP In a small saucepan, combine 3 smashed and coarsely chopped fresh lemongrass stalks with 1 cup of sugar, 1½ cups of water and 1 tablespoon of light corn syrup and bring to a boil. Simmer over low heat until the syrup coats the back of a spoon, about 30 minutes. Let the syrup cool, then strain and refrigerate for up to 5 days. Makes 8 ounces of syrup.

Perfect Sky

The Shore Club hotel's sprawling, mostly open-air bar has four separate lounges. Seating in the 2,500-square-foot RedRoom Garden includes wooden daybeds surrounded by bougainvillea.

Sky Bar • Miami

Ice
1½ ounces raspberry vodka
1 ounce peach nectar or syrup
½ ounce peach schnapps
¼ to ½ ounce fresh lime juice
1 ounce chilled ginger ale

Fill a cocktail shaker with ice. Add the vodka, peach nectar, schnapps and fresh lime juice and shake well. Strain into a chilled martini glass and top with the chilled ginger ale.

Health

Health is an improbably delicious combination from "liquid chef" Ryan Magarian. "I can't put my finger on the exact inspiration," he says. "Yellow bell pepper and vanilla vodka just sounded good together one day."

Jäger • Kirkland, WA

One 2-inch grapefruit wedge
Two 3-by-½-inch strips of yellow bell pepper, plus 1 thin strip for garnish
2 large basil sprigs
1½ ounces vanilla vodka
1 ounce Simple Syrup (P. 17)
½ ounce fresh lemon juice
½ ounce fresh lime juice
Ice

In a cocktail shaker, muddle the grapefruit with the yellow pepper strips. Tear and bruise the basil sprigs. Add the basil, vodka, Simple Syrup and citrus juices to the shaker, fill with ice and shake vigorously. Strain into a chilled martini glass and garnish with the thin yellow pepper strip.

JADE COCKTAIL
Jade Bar, San Francisco

Jade Cocktail

Jade Bar • San Francisco

A 20-foot waterfall plunges from Jade Bar's upstairs loft to its avocado-green basement.

Ice
- 2 ounces pineapple juice
- 1½ ounces vanilla vodka
- 1 ounce fresh lime juice
- ½ ounce Midori
- ½ ounce fresh lemon juice
- ½ ounce Simple Syrup (P. 17)

Fill a cocktail shaker with ice. Add all of the ingredients, shake well and strain into a large chilled martini glass.

Pomegranate Martini

Union Bar and Grille • Boston

The leather-fronted bar and tooled-leather wall panel in the bar area recall this South End restaurant's past life as a leather warehouse.

Ice
- 1½ ounces vanilla vodka
- 1½ teaspoons peach schnapps
- ½ ounce fresh lemon juice
- 1½ teaspoons Simple Syrup (P. 17)
- 1½ ounces pomegranate juice
- ½ ounce chilled Sprite
- 1 lime wheel

Fill a cocktail shaker with ice. Add all of the ingredients except the Sprite and lime wheel and shake well. Strain into a chilled martini glass, top with the Sprite and garnish with the lime wheel.

Sex in the Bathroom

d.b.a. bartender Bethanny Lemanski created this drink in honor of the famously bawdy behavior of New Orleans revelers.

d.b.a. • New Orleans

Ice
- 2 ounces vanilla vodka
- 2 ounces raspberry vodka
- 1½ teaspoons cranberry juice
- 1½ teaspoons pineapple juice
- 2 ounces chilled ginger beer
- 2 maraschino cherries

Fill a cocktail shaker with ice. Add the vodkas and fruit juices and shake well. Strain into a large chilled martini glass, top with the ginger beer and garnish with the cherries.

Blueberry Bliss

This bistro's 8,000-square-foot veranda offers a sweeping view of Charleston Harbor and includes a reflecting pool with an 18-foot geyser.

Zinc Bistro & Bar • Mount Pleasant, SC

- ½ cup fresh blueberries

Ice
- 1½ ounces vanilla vodka
- 1 ounce white cranberry juice
- 2 ounces chilled ginger ale
- 1 lime wedge
- 1 vanilla bean

In a cocktail shaker, muddle the blueberries, then fill the shaker with ice. Add the vodka and cranberry juice and shake well. Strain into a highball glass over ice and top with the ginger ale and a squeeze of lime. Stir well and garnish with the vanilla bean.

Apples & Oranges

Tangerine • Philadelphia

Tangerine's romantic 60-seat lounge is lit by six candle-filled chandeliers and shrouded by floor-to-ceiling velvet curtains.

1 orange wedge and Tang (optional)
Ice
1½ ounces orange vodka
¾ ounce sour apple liqueur
1 orange twist

If desired, moisten the outer rim of a martini glass with the orange wedge and coat lightly with Tang. Fill a cocktail shaker with ice. Add the vodka and sour apple liqueur and shake well. Strain into the martini glass and garnish with the orange twist.

Indigo Martini

Indigo • Honolulu

The lounge at this East-West fusion restaurant in Honolulu's Chinatown is known for guest DJs who spin five nights a week.

Ice
1½ ounces orange vodka
1 ounce blue curaçao
1 ounce fresh lime juice
½ ounce Simple Syrup (P. 17)
1 orange wheel

Fill a cocktail shaker with ice. Add the vodka, curaçao, lime juice and Simple Syrup and shake well. Strain into a chilled martini glass and garnish with the orange wheel.

LUSH
MidCity Cuisine,
Atlanta

Rose Martini

Seating at Moda's riverside outdoor lounge includes bright orange plastic stools shaped like enormous doorknobs.

Moda • Providence

Ice
3 ounces vodka
1 ounce rose syrup
Dash of Angostura bitters
Organic rose petals

Fill a cocktail shaker with ice. Add the vodka, rose syrup and bitters and shake well. Strain into a chilled martini glass and garnish with rose petals.

Lush

Chef-owner Shaun Doty and bar manager Jacki Schmidt created Lush as an aperitif, but it's become a popular nightcap among theater-goers from the neighboring Ansley Park Playhouse.

MidCity Cuisine • Atlanta

Ice
1 ounce vodka, preferably Ciroc
½ ounce Grand Marnier
1½ teaspoons elderflower syrup
2 ounces chilled rosé Champagne
1 small bunch of Champagne grapes, frozen

Fill a cocktail shaker with ice. Add the vodka, Grand Marnier and elderflower syrup and shake well. Strain into a chilled martini glass, top with the Champagne and garnish with the grapes.

Bella Martini

Santacafé • Santa Fe

Santacafé is in the historic home of 19th-century priest and politician José Manuel Gallegos, New Mexico's first congressional representative.

Ice
1½ ounces vodka
1 ounce Pear Syrup (below)
1 to 2 ounces chilled Champagne
1 lemon twist

Fill a cocktail shaker with ice. Add the vodka and Pear Syrup and shake vigorously. Strain into a chilled martini glass, top with the Champagne and garnish with the lemon twist.

PEAR SYRUP In a small saucepan, simmer 8 ounces of pear nectar or juice over moderately high heat until reduced by half, about 20 minutes. Let cool, then refrigerate for up to 5 days. Makes 4 ounces of syrup.

Coconut Martini

Pho Republique • Boston

While the Coconut Martini is served in a martini glass, other drinks at this pan-Asian restaurant are presented in bamboo-shaped glass tumblers or large clay pots with straws.

Ice
3 ounces vodka
2 ounces cream of coconut from a well-shaken can
1 mint leaf

Fill a cocktail shaker with ice. Add the vodka and cream of coconut and shake vigorously. Strain into a chilled martini glass and garnish with the mint leaf.

Strawberry Caipiroska

The vodka-based caipiroska is a Russified twist on Brazil's classic caipirinha, made with rum. Bahía tweaks the recipe further by replacing the traditional lime with strawberry.

Bahía • Miami

1 heaping cup strawberries, hulled
1 tablespoon sugar
Ice
2 ounces vodka

In a cocktail shaker, muddle all but 1 of the strawberries with the sugar until juicy. Add enough ice to fill a rocks glass and top with the vodka. Shake briefly to chill, then pour into a rocks glass. Garnish with the reserved strawberry.

Lychee Martini

Housed in a former bank, this French-Indian restaurant features an enormous woven wood Hookah Den, which has been used exclusively for drinking and dining since Boston's 2003 smoking ban.

Mantra • Boston

Ice
3 ounces lychee nectar or juice
2 ounces vodka
1½ teaspoons fresh lemon juice
1½ teaspoons Simple Syrup (P. 17)

Fill a cocktail shaker with ice. Add the lychee nectar, vodka, lemon juice and Simple Syrup and shake well, then strain into a chilled martini glass.

ROOF GARDEN
Grace, Los Angeles

Roof Garden

Grace • Los Angeles

This refreshing cocktail is made with thyme and mint, two herbs that thrive in urban rooftop gardens.

- 15 mint leaves, plus 1 mint sprig for garnish
- 2 thyme sprigs
- 2 teaspoons sugar
- 2 ounces vodka
- 1 ounce fresh lemon juice
- 1 ounce Simple Syrup (P. 17)
- Ice
- 1 to 2 ounces chilled club soda

In a cocktail shaker, muddle the mint leaves with the thyme and sugar. Add the vodka, lemon juice, Simple Syrup and ice and shake well. Strain into a highball glass over ice, top with the club soda and garnish with the mint sprig.

Late Blossom

Lantern • Chapel Hill, NC

Almost everything here is house-made: Brother and sister chef-owners Andrea and Brendan Reusing cure the Chinese-style hams, while pastry chef April McGreger makes pistachio fortune cookies and orange-clove bathroom soap.

- ½ teaspoon orange-flower water
- Ice
- 1½ ounces potato vodka
- 1¼ ounces lychee nectar or juice
- 1½ teaspoons Lillet Blanc
- 1 fresh lychee, partially peeled

Rinse a chilled martini glass with the orange-flower water. Fill a cocktail shaker with ice. Add the vodka, lychee nectar and Lillet and shake well. Strain into the martini glass and garnish with the lychee.

Gimlet

Matchbox • Chicago

Made with either vodka or the more traditional gin, the lime-spiked gimlet was created by an early 20th-century British naval surgeon to combat scurvy.

Ice
- 3 ounces vodka
- 1¼ ounces fresh lime juice
- ½ large pasteurized egg white (optional)
- 1 heaping teaspoon powdered sugar

Fill a cocktail shaker with ice. Add all of the ingredients, shake vigorously and strain into a chilled martini glass.

Bloody Mary

Fox & Hounds Tavern • St. Louis

Bartender Mark Pollman owns more than 5,000 cocktail-related books and is himself the author of one called *Bottled Wisdom*, a collection of 1,008 quotations about drinking.

- 5 ounces tomato juice
- 1½ ounces vodka
- Juice of 2 lime wedges
- ½ teaspoon finely grated fresh horseradish
- 2 or 3 dashes of Worcestershire sauce
- 3 or 4 drops of Tabasco sauce
- Pinch of salt
- Pinch of celery salt
- Small pinch of cayenne pepper
- Ice

Combine all of the ingredients in a pint glass. Pour the drink back and forth between the pint glass and a cocktail shaker four times, then pour the Bloody Mary into a highball glass over ice.

Tomato Water Bloody Mary

This Old Town restaurant occupies a restored 18th-century warehouse. Bar manager Todd Thrasher lightens the Bloody Mary by replacing tomato juice with "tomato water."

Restaurant Eve • Alexandria, VA

MAKES 4 DRINKS

Ice
- 16 ounces Tomato Water (below)
- 6 ounces pepper vodka
- 4 savory sprigs

Fill 4 highball glasses with ice. Add 4 ounces of Tomato Water and 1½ ounces of vodka to each glass. Stir well and garnish each glass with a savory sprig.

TOMATO WATER In a food processor, combine 4 large beefsteak tomatoes cut into chunks with ½ serrano chile, ⅛ red onion, 1 coarsely chopped 2-inch stalk of lemongrass and a large pinch of salt; puree until smooth. Pour the puree into a cheesecloth-lined strainer set over a bowl and refrigerate overnight. Discard the pulp. Add 2 ounces of fresh orange juice to the mixture and refrigerate for up to 1 day. Makes 16 ounces of Tomato Water.

THE VAMP
Brasa, Seattle

The Vamp

Two locally famous women are in charge here: Mi Suk Ahn is behind the bar and Tamara Murphy (an F&W Best New Chef 1994) is in the kitchen.

Brasa • Seattle

Splash of bourbon
Ice
1 ounce vodka
½ ounce ruby port
½ ounce crème de cassis

Rinse a chilled martini glass with the bourbon. Fill a cocktail shaker with ice. Add the vodka, port and crème de cassis, shake well and strain into the martini glass.

Bitter Queen

The Martini Bar's 1940s terrazzo floor features a mosaic in the shape of a martini glass.

Martini Bar at the Raleigh Hotel • Miami

Ice
2 ounces vodka
1 ounce Campari
1 ounce limoncello
2 ounces chilled fresh orange juice
1 lime wheel

Fill a cocktail shaker with ice. Add the vodka, Campari and limoncello and shake well. Strain into a large chilled martini glass, top with the orange juice and garnish with the lime wheel.

CHEVAL
Loa, New Orleans

Cheval

Based on the Moscow Mule, a 1940s drink developed to promote Smirnoff vodka, Loa's Cheval uses muddled cucumber.

Loa • New Orleans

¼ seedless cucumber, thinly sliced
2 lime quarters
Ice
1½ ounces vodka
1½ to 2 ounces chilled ginger beer

In a cocktail shaker, muddle all but 1 of the cucumber slices with the lime quarters. Add ice and the vodka, shake well and strain into an ice-filled highball glass. Top with the ginger beer and garnish with the remaining cucumber slice.

Einstein

Bar manager Jason Winters came up with this cocktail to showcase Scotland's superpremium, exceptionally smooth Brilliant vodka—hence the drink's name.

Falcon • Hollywood, CA

Splash of añejo tequila
Ice
3 ounces vodka
1 orange twist and 1 lemon twist

Rinse a chilled martini glass with the tequila. Fill a cocktail shaker with ice. Add the vodka, shake vigorously and strain into the martini glass. Garnish with the orange and lemon twists.

Cardamom Cooler

Chapel • Seattle

This mortuary–turned–cocktail lounge specializes in house-infused vodkas and syrups—like the cardamom syrup in this twist on vodka and soda.

Ice
2 ounces vodka
1 ounce Cardamom Syrup (below)
1½ teaspoons fresh lime juice
1½ teaspoons fresh lemon juice
2 ounces chilled club soda

Fill a cocktail shaker with ice. Add the vodka, Cardamom Syrup and citrus juices and shake well. Strain into an ice-filled highball glass and top with the club soda.

CARDAMOM SYRUP In a heatproof bowl, steep 1 heaping tablespoon of crushed cardamom pods in 8 ounces of hot Simple Syrup (P. 17) for at least 2 hours. Strain and refrigerate for up to 5 days. Makes 8 ounces of syrup.

Asian Blonde

RoHan Lounge • San Francisco

The cocktails here are made exclusively with *soju*, a vodka-like Korean spirit distilled from rice, barley and sweet potato.

Ice
- **3 ounces *soju***
- **3 ounces fresh orange juice**
- **½ ounce fresh lemon juice**
- **½ ounce fresh lime juice**
- **½ ounce fresh carrot juice**

Fill a highball glass with ice. Add the *soju* and citrus juices, then top with the carrot juice.

Maiden's Blush

Moosh • Dallas

The drinks at Moosh are shaken with large chunks of ice chipped from a huge block; the chunks melt more slowly than cubes do, diluting the drinks less.

Ice
- **3 ounces *soju***
- **¾ ounce triple sec**
- **½ ounce fresh lemon juice**
- **½ teaspoon grenadine**

Fill a cocktail shaker with ice. Add the *soju*, triple sec, lemon juice and grenadine, shake well and strain into a chilled martini glass.

THAI MARTINI (LEFT), P. 65
Cuchi Cuchi, Cambridge, MA
STONE WALL, P. 76
Silverleaf Tavern, New York City

RUM

Mojito

Martini Bar at the Raleigh Hotel • Miami

Esther Williams shot some of her most famous 1940s movie scenes in the palm-lined swimming pool at this refurbished Art Deco hotel, which was recently purchased by André Balazs.

8 mint sprigs
3 lime quarters, plus 1 lime wedge for garnish
½ ounce Simple Syrup **(P. 17)**
Ice
2 ounces light rum
1 ounce chilled club soda
Dash of Angostura bitters

In a cocktail shaker, muddle 7 of the mint sprigs with the 3 lime quarters and Simple Syrup. Add ice and the rum; shake well. Strain into an ice-filled highball glass and top with the soda and bitters. Garnish with the lime wedge and remaining mint sprig.

Champagne Mojito

Flow • Denver

Rich aged rum and Champagne replace light rum and club soda in this refined twist on the mojito.

15 mint leaves
1½ ounces Simple Syrup **(P. 17)**
Ice
2 ounces aged rum
1 ounce fresh lime juice
2 ounces chilled Champagne
1 orange twist

In a highball glass, muddle the mint leaves with the Simple Syrup. Fill the glass with ice, add the rum and lime juice and stir gently. Top with the chilled Champagne and garnish with the orange twist.

Coco Mojito

Mirasol • St. Louis

Co-owners Brendan and Brian Marsden and their former bartender Nhat Nguyen, a Miami Beach transplant, developed this frothy cocktail.

12 mint leaves
½ ounce fresh lime juice
2 ounces coconut rum
½ ounce Simple Syrup (P. 17)
1 ounce cream of coconut from a well-shaken can
Ice
1 to 2 ounces chilled club soda

In a cocktail shaker, muddle the mint with the lime juice. Add the rum, Simple Syrup, cream of coconut and ice and shake vigorously. Strain into an ice-filled highball glass and top with the club soda.

Blueberry Mojito

St. Joe's Bar • New Orleans

Folk art crosses hang from the ceiling and church pews surround the pool table at this quirky bar.

10 mint leaves, plus 1 mint sprig for garnish
10 blueberries
¾ ounce Simple Syrup (P. 17)
Ice
1½ ounces gold rum
1 ounce fresh lime juice
1 ounce chilled club soda
1 ounce chilled Sprite

In a cocktail shaker, muddle the mint leaves, blueberries and Simple Syrup. Fill with ice, add the rum and lime juice and shake well. Strain into an ice-filled highball glass, top with the club soda and Sprite and garnish with the mint sprig.

Kiwi Mojito

Washington Square • Philadelphia

In warm weather, this restaurant serves cocktails and small bites in intimate garden alcoves lined with multicolored tiles designed by Todd Oldham.

½ cup peeled and coarsely chopped kiwi (1 medium kiwi)
3 mint leaves
½ ounce Mint Syrup (below)
Ice
2 ounces light rum
½ ounce fresh lime juice
1 lime wheel

In a mini food processor, puree the kiwi until smooth, then refrigerate until needed. In a cocktail shaker, muddle the mint leaves with the Mint Syrup. Fill the shaker with ice, then add the rum, lime juice and kiwi puree. Shake vigorously and strain into an ice-filled highball glass. Garnish with the lime wheel.

MINT SYRUP In a small saucepan, bring ½ cup of water and ½ cup of sugar to a boil. Remove from the heat and add 10 whole torn mint sprigs. Steep for at least 2 hours, then strain and refrigerate for up to 5 days. Makes about 5 ounces of syrup.

Ride Sally Ride

JP American Bistro • Minneapolis

Named in honor of astronaut Sally K. Ride, this drink is served in a Tang-rimmed martini glass.

1 orange wedge and Tang (optional)
Ice
2 ounces fresh orange juice
1½ ounces orange rum
½ ounce peach schnapps
½ ounce fresh lemon juice
1 orange wheel

If desired, moisten the outer rim of a martini glass with the orange wedge and coat lightly with Tang. Fill a cocktail shaker with ice. Add the orange juice, rum, schnapps and lemon juice and shake well. Strain into the martini glass and garnish with the orange wheel.

Golden Buddha

Parallel 33 • San Diego

The globetrotting dinner and cocktail menus here celebrate the ingredients of Morocco, Lebanon, India, China and Japan, all places that share San Diego's latitude, the 33rd parallel.

1 lemon wedge and sugar
Ice
2 ounces spiced rum
2 ounces chilled ginger beer
1 tablespoon finely chopped, candied ginger

Moisten the outer rim of a martini glass with the lemon wedge and coat lightly with sugar. Fill a cocktail shaker with ice. Add all of the remaining ingredients, shake well and strain into the martini glass.

SPICE
Jäger, Kirkland, WA

Spice

Jäger • Kirkland, WA

Noted mixologist Ryan Magarian plays up food-and-cocktail pairings. His Spice cocktail goes well with the Jägerschnitzel, a breaded pork cutlet served with mushroom sauce and spaetzle.

Ice
2 large mint sprigs, torn and bruised
1½ ounces spiced rum
1 ounce pear nectar or juice
¾ ounce fresh lime juice
¾ ounce Simple Syrup (P. 17)
Pinch of freshly grated nutmeg
1 thin slice of pear

Fill a cocktail shaker with ice. Add all of the ingredients except the pear slice and shake well. Strain into a chilled martini glass and garnish with the pear slice.

Thai Martini

Cuchi Cuchi • Cambridge, MA

This drink was inspired by a Thai soup recipe made with apple and coconut milk.

½ Granny Smith apple, chopped, plus 1 thin slice for garnish
1 teaspoon minced lemongrass (tender inner bulb only)
Ice
2½ ounces coconut rum
1 ounce sour apple liqueur

In a cocktail shaker, muddle the chopped apple with the lemongrass. Fill the shaker with ice. Add the rum and sour apple liqueur and shake well. Strain into a chilled martini glass and garnish with the apple slice.

FAHRENHEIT 5
Degrees,
Washington, D.C.

Fahrenheit 5

Degrees • Washington, D.C.

Charismatic bartender Michael Brown teaches drink-making at monthly workshops.

Ice
¾ ounce coconut rum
¾ ounce Grand Marnier
1¼ ounces cranberry juice
¾ ounce pineapple juice
Splash of chilled Sprite

Fill a cocktail shaker with ice. Add the rum, Grand Marnier and fruit juices and shake well. Strain into a chilled martini glass and top with the Sprite.

Orchid

Bluehour • Portland, OR

Originally created with the Myers's rum left over from a private party, this riff on the mai tai is served in an enormous 23-ounce snifter and garnished with an orchid.

½ ounce unsweetened coconut water
½ ounce Simple Syrup (P. 17)
1½ ounces light rum
2 ounces fresh lemon juice
1 ounce fresh orange juice
Crushed ice
1 ounce dark rum, preferably Myers's
1 edible orchid (optional)

In a large brandy snifter, stir together the coconut water and Simple Syrup. Stir in the light rum, lemon juice and orange juice. Add enough crushed ice to fill the snifter halfway, then top with the dark rum. If desired, garnish with the orchid.

Daiquiri

Porcupine • New York City

This century-old classic was invented in the seaside village of Daiquirí, near Santiago de Cuba.

Ice
1½ ounces light rum
½ ounce fresh lime juice
1 teaspoon Simple Syrup (P. 17)

Fill a cocktail shaker with ice. Add the rum, lime juice and Simple Syrup and shake vigorously. Strain into a chilled martini glass.

La Floridita

Mona's • Seattle

Mona's Spanish and Portuguese tapas and twice-weekly live bossa nova are complemented by cocktails like this one, based on a drink once served at La Florida, a famous Havana bar of the 1930s.

Ice
1½ ounces light rum
1½ ounces sweet vermouth
½ teaspoon white crème de cacao
1½ ounces fresh lime juice
½ teaspoon grenadine
1 pineapple spear

Fill a cocktail shaker with ice. Add all of the ingredients except the pineapple spear and shake well. Strain into an ice-filled highball glass and garnish with the pineapple spear.

Avocado Daiquiri

820 • Portland, OR

An odd-sounding drink, this twist on a banana daiquiri has become one of owner Lucy Brennan's most popular creations.

- **2 ounces light rum**
- **2 ounces dark rum**
- **2 ounces Simple Syrup (P. 17)**
- **1 ounce fresh lemon juice**
- **¼ Hass avocado, peeled and sliced**
- **1½ teaspoons half-and-half**
- **1 cup crushed ice**

In a blender, combine all of the ingredients. Blend until the drink is completely smooth, then pour into a red wine glass.

Nuevo Cuba Libre

Cuba Libre • Philadelphia

Built to resemble Old Havana of the 1940s, this weathered Old City restaurant feels like a movie set, with tall palms, oversized ceiling fans and servers dressed in guayabera shirts.

- **Ice**
- **1¼ ounces light rum**
- **¾ ounce gin**
- **5 to 6 ounces chilled Coca-Cola**
- **½ ounce fresh lime juice**
- **2 dashes of Angostura bitters**
- **1 lime wheel**

Fill a highball glass with ice and add the rum, gin and Coca-Cola. Top with the lime juice and bitters, stir well and garnish with the lime wheel.

GOSLING'S SIDECAR
The Slanted Door,
San Francisco

Negril Tea

Automatic Slim's Tonga Club • Memphis

Chef and owner Karen Blockman Carrier named this drink for the Jamaican town of Negril, where she learned Caribbean cooking (and rum appreciation) from squatters living on the beach.

Ice
- 2 ounces dark rum
- 1 ounce spiced rum
- 1 ounce fresh lemon juice
- 1 ounce Simple Syrup (P. 17)
- ½ ounce fresh lime juice
- 1 lemon wheel

Fill a cocktail shaker with ice. Add all of the ingredients except the lemon wheel and shake well. Strain into an ice-filled highball glass and garnish with the lemon wheel.

Gosling's Sidecar

The Slanted Door • San Francisco

"I was having a hard time turning people on to the traditional sidecar made with brandy," says bar manager Thad Vogler. "So I switched to dark rum, which is soft and sweet and much more of a crowd-pleaser."

- 1 lemon wedge (optional)
- ½ teaspoon sugar, plus more for rimming the glass (optional)
- ¾ ounce fresh lemon juice

Ice
- 1½ ounces dark rum, preferably Gosling's
- ¾ ounce triple sec
- 1 lemon twist (optional)

If desired, moisten the outer rim of a martini glass with the lemon wedge and coat lightly with sugar. In a cocktail shaker, stir the ½ teaspoon of sugar with the lemon juice. Fill the shaker with ice, add the rum and triple sec and shake well. Strain into the martini glass and, if desired, garnish with the lemon twist.

Mai Tai

House Without a Key • Honolulu

Created by restaurateur Victor "Trader Vic" Bergeron in 1944 to showcase an exceptional aged rum, the original mai tai recipe called for rock candy syrup, which is sweeter than simple syrup.

Ice
- **¾ ounce gold rum**
- **¾ ounce dark rum**
- **1½ teaspoons orange curaçao**
- **1½ teaspoons orgeat syrup**
- **1½ teaspoons Simple Syrup (P. 17)**
- **1¼ ounces fresh lemon juice**
- **½ ounce overproof rum**
- **1 lime wheel, 1 sugarcane stick, 1 mint sprig and 1 edible orchid (all optional)**

Fill a highball glass with ice. Add all of the ingredients except the overproof rum and garnishes; stir, then top with the overproof rum. If desired, garnish with the lime wheel, sugarcane stick, mint sprig and orchid.

Stonefruit Sling

Fiamma Trattoria • Scottsdale

"Sling" most often refers to a fruit punch–style combination of spirits, liqueurs and citrus juices shaken and served on ice. This version was created by molecular biologist–turned–mixologist Eben Klemm.

Ice
- **1 ounce gold rum**
- **½ ounce cherry liqueur**
- **½ ounce peach schnapps**
- **½ ounce apricot nectar or juice**
- **1½ teaspoons fresh lemon juice**
- **1½ teaspoons Simple Syrup (P. 17)**
- **1 to 2 ounces chilled ginger ale**

Fill a cocktail shaker with ice. Add all of the ingredients except the ginger ale. Shake well, strain into an ice-filled highball glass and top with the ginger ale.

Mount Lychee

Under the Volcano • Houston

Owner Pete Mitchell's wide-ranging taste in music accounts for this bar's renowned jukebox, which plays everything from Hank Williams to The Roots to N.E.R.D.

4 canned lychees, plus ½ ounce syrup from the can
1 large lemon twist
2 ounces gold rum
Ice

In a cocktail shaker, muddle the lychees with their syrup and the lemon twist. Add the rum and enough ice to fill a highball glass. Shake well and pour—do not strain—into the glass.

Caribbean Cowboy Cocktail

Johnny V • Ft. Lauderdale

This cocktail's name refers to its combination of Latin and Southwestern ingredients—a hallmark of chef and owner Johnny Vinczencz's cooking style.

1 small lime wedge and chili powder
2 ounces gold rum
2 ounces mango nectar or juice
2 ounces fresh lime juice
2½ ounces lychee nectar or juice
3 mint leaves
Ice
1 slice of star fruit (carambola)

Moisten the outer rim of a large martini glass with the lime and coat with chili powder. In a blender, combine all of the remaining ingredients except the ice and star fruit; blend well. Pour into a cocktail shaker filled with ice. Shake well, strain into the martini glass and garnish with the star fruit.

STAR OF INDIA
Monsoon, Chicago

Gansevoort Fizz

5 Ninth • New York City

Mixologist and cocktail historian David Wondrich adapted this recipe from a 1930s drink called the MacKinnon after the family that owned Drambuie.

Ice
- 2 ounces aged rum
- 1 ounce Drambuie
- 1 ounce fresh lemon juice
- 2 dashes of bitters, preferably Peychaud's
- 2 ounces chilled club soda

Fill a cocktail shaker with ice. Add the rum, Drambuie, lemon juice and bitters and shake well. Strain into an ice-filled highball glass and top with the club soda.

Star of India

Monsoon • Chicago

Framed quotations from Eastern philosophers ("Harmony is the real essence of marriage") line the walls of this elegant Indian-Asian restaurant.

Ice
- 1½ ounces aged rum
- ½ ounce triple sec
- ¾ ounce passion fruit nectar or juice
- 1½ teaspoons sambuca

Splash of chilled Sprite
- 1 organic rose petal (optional)

Fill a cocktail shaker with ice. Add all of the ingredients except the Sprite and rose petal and shake well. Strain into a chilled martini glass and top with the Sprite. If desired, garnish with the rose petal.

Guava Mai Tai

Flatiron Lounge • New York City

At this Art Deco–inspired lounge, mixologist Julie Reiner hosts summertime Sunday-night tiki parties complete with her version of the mai tai.

Ice
1½ ounces aged rum
¾ ounce orange curaçao
¾ ounce fresh lime juice
¾ ounce fresh orange juice
¾ ounce guava nectar or juice
1½ teaspoons orgeat syrup
1 pineapple spear

Fill a cocktail shaker with ice. Add all of the ingredients except the pineapple. Shake well, strain into an ice-filled highball glass and garnish with the pineapple spear.

Stone Wall

Silverleaf Tavern • New York City

The drinks at this Kimpton hotel restaurant are the work of cocktail master Dale DeGroff, famous for his showmanship at New York City's Rainbow Room from 1987 to 1999.

One 1-inch piece of fresh ginger, peeled and thinly sliced
1½ teaspoons Simple Syrup (P. 17)
1½ ounces aged rum
1½ ounces apple cider
Ice
1½ ounces chilled ginger beer
1 lime wedge and 1 slice of apple

In a cocktail shaker, muddle the sliced ginger with the Simple Syrup. Add the rum, cider and ice and shake well. Strain into an ice-filled rocks glass and top with the ginger beer. Garnish with the lime wedge and apple slice.

Caipirinha

Enrico Banducci's restaurant has been a Bay Area mainstay since it opened in 1958. The bartenders are famous for their aggressive muddling.

Enrico's Sidewalk Cafe • San Francisco

- ½ lime, cut into wedges
- 2 teaspoons sugar
- Ice
- 2 ounces cachaça

In a rocks glass, muddle the lime with the sugar. Fill the glass with ice and add the cachaça. Transfer to a cocktail shaker, shake well and pour back into the rocks glass.

Batida

An in-house sugarcane press provides fresh sugarcane juice, known as *guarapo,* for everything from mojitos to house-cured pork loin.

Ceiba • Washington, D.C.

- Ice
- 2 ounces cachaça
- 1 ounce tamarind syrup
- ½ ounce passion fruit nectar or juice
- ½ ounce fresh lemon juice
- ½ ounce fresh lime juice

Fill a cocktail shaker with ice. Add all of the ingredients, shake well and strain into a chilled martini glass.

LYCHEE GIMLET, P. 88
Circolo, San Francisco

GIN

Martini

Bar Marmont • Los Angeles

This low-key bar adjacent to the Chateau Marmont serves its martini shaken, not stirred, with an individual shaker holding the extra.

1½ teaspoons dry vermouth
Ice
3 ounces gin
2 green olives

Swirl the vermouth in a chilled martini glass. Fill a cocktail shaker with ice, add the gin and shake vigorously. Strain into the martini glass and garnish with the olives.

Lotus Martini

Crave • Dearborn, MI

The exotic decor at this 3,700-square-foot Asian-Mediterranean restaurant and nightclub includes an electric blue jellyfish aquarium.

Ice
1¾ ounces gin
1½ ounces lychee nectar or juice
1½ teaspoons blue curaçao
1½ teaspoons grenadine
1 mint leaf

Fill a cocktail shaker with ice. Add all of the ingredients except the mint leaf and shake well. Strain into a chilled martini glass and garnish with the mint leaf.

Strawberry-Basil Martini

The unusual combination of strawberry and basil in this martini is the work of El Salvador–born mixologist José Zepeda.

Fix • Las Vegas

- 3 strawberries, plus 1 thin slice of strawberry for garnish
- 3 basil leaves
- ½ ounce Simple Syrup (P. 17)
- Ice
- 1 ounce gin, preferably Tanqueray No. Ten
- 1 ounce vodka
- ½ ounce fresh lime juice

In a cocktail shaker, muddle the strawberries with the basil leaves and Simple Syrup. Add ice and the remaining ingredients and shake well. Strain into a chilled martini glass and garnish with the strawberry slice.

Blue Ice Martini

Though you won't see The Peabody hotel's famed ducks (they stay in the lobby), The Corner Bar offers more than 40 martinis and live music courtesy of blues singer Blind Mississippi Morris.

The Corner Bar • Memphis

- Ice
- 2 ounces gin
- 1½ teaspoons white crème de menthe

Fill a cocktail shaker with ice. Add the gin and white crème de menthe, shake well and strain into a chilled martini glass.

BLUEBERRY COBBLER
No. 9 Park,
Boston

Retrotini

Compound • Atlanta

Occupying a former high-end car showroom, this sleek, airy, Asian-inspired club features an outdoor terrace and a glowing ornamental pool.

Ice
2 ounces gin
1 ounce triple sec
1 ounce white cranberry juice

Fill a cocktail shaker with ice. Add the gin, triple sec and cranberry juice, shake well and strain into a chilled martini glass.

Blueberry Cobbler

No. 9 Park • Boston

Bar managers Ryan McGrale and John Gertsen develop seasonal variations on the cobbler, a pre-Prohibition cocktail made with sugar and fresh fruit—blueberries in summer, tart Concord grapes in autumn.

¼ cup fresh blueberries
1 small lime wedge
1½ teaspoons sugar
1½ ounces gin
Ice
2 ounces chilled club soda

In a cocktail shaker, muddle 15 of the blueberries with the lime wedge and sugar. Add the gin and ice and shake well. Strain into a highball glass half-filled with ice, top with the club soda and garnish with the remaining blueberries.

Pompano

Trina • Ft. Lauderdale

Mixologist Nick Mautone, who made his name at New York City's Gramercy Tavern, developed the drinks for this Mediterranean restaurant in The Atlantic hotel.

Ice
- 2 ounces gin, preferably Tanqueray No. Ten
- 1½ ounces fresh grapefruit juice
- ½ ounce sweet vermouth
- 1 dash of Angostura or orange bitters

Fill a cocktail shaker with ice. Add all of the ingredients, shake well and strain into a chilled martini glass.

Fahrenheit Fizz

Fahrenheit • Cleveland

Fahrenheit's menu is arranged according to the temperatures at which items are prepared: 600 degrees for pizzas, 1,000 for steaks and seafood and 36 for cocktails.

Ice
- 3 ounces gin
- 1 ounce fresh lemon juice
- ½ ounce Chambord
- 2 teaspoons powdered sugar
- 1 ounce chilled Champagne
- 1 lemon twist

Fill a cocktail shaker with ice. Add all of the ingredients except the Champagne and lemon twist and shake well. Strain into a chilled martini glass, top with the Champagne and garnish with the twist.

Junipero 102

This drink uses the intensely juniper-flavored Junípero Gin from San Francisco's Anchor Distilling Company. The cocktail's name refers to the time it was perfected: 1:02 A.M.

Tempo • Brooklyn, NY

Ice
- 2 ounces gin
- 1 ounce fresh lime juice
- 1½ teaspoons Simple Syrup (P. 17)
- 2 ounces chilled Moscato d'Asti
- 1 lime twist

Fill a cocktail shaker with ice. Add the gin, lime juice and Simple Syrup and shake well. Strain into a chilled martini glass, top with the Moscato and garnish with the lime twist.

Princeton

Turn-of-the-century wainscoting and a 75-year-old pressed tin ceiling give this Cambridge bar a vintage feel, as do the drinks that owner Patrick Sullivan draws from his collection of old cocktail books.

B-Side Lounge • Cambridge, MA

Ice
- 2 ounces gin
- 1 ounce ruby port
- 2 dashes of Angostura or orange bitters
- 1 orange twist

Fill two-thirds of a pint glass or cocktail shaker with ice. Add the gin, port and bitters and stir until completely chilled, about 30 seconds. Strain into a chilled martini glass and garnish with the orange twist.

ROSEMARY SALTY DOG
Enoteca Vin, Raleigh, NC

Rosemary Salty Dog

Chef Ashley Christensen adds muddled fresh rosemary to her version of the gin–and–grapefruit juice classic.

Enoteca Vin • Raleigh, NC

1 grapefruit wedge and kosher salt
One 1-inch piece of rosemary sprig, plus 1 sprig for garnish
½ teaspoon sugar
2 ounces fresh red grapefruit juice
1½ ounces gin
Ice

Moisten the outer rim of a martini glass with the grapefruit wedge and coat lightly with salt. In a cocktail shaker, muddle the 1-inch rosemary sprig with the sugar. Add the grapefruit juice, gin and ice and shake vigorously. Strain into the martini glass and garnish with the rosemary sprig.

Major Tom

Many of the cocktails at Sputnik have a Soviet theme, with names like Proletariat, Marx and Yuri Gagarin.

Sputnik • Denver

Ice
2 ounces gin
2 ounces guava nectar or juice
1 mint sprig, torn and bruised

Fill a cocktail shaker with ice. Add all of the ingredients, shake well and strain into a chilled martini glass.

Lychee Gimlet

Circolo • San Francisco

Lychee nectar balances the tartness of fresh lime juice in this Asian-Peruvian restaurant's take on the gimlet.

- 1 lime wedge and sugar
- Ice
- 1½ ounces gin
- ½ ounce triple sec
- 1½ ounces fresh lime juice
- 1½ teaspoons Simple Syrup (P. 17)
- 2 ounces lychee nectar or juice
- 1 lychee, preferably fresh (optional)

Moisten the outer rim of a large martini glass with the lime wedge and coat lightly with sugar. Fill a cocktail shaker with ice. Add the gin, triple sec, lime juice, Simple Syrup and lychee nectar and shake well. Strain into the martini glass; if desired, garnish with the lychee.

Pantelleria

Pace • New York City

Inspired by the North African influences in Sicilian cooking, this twist on the gimlet adds fragrant orange-flower water.

- Ice
- 3 ounces gin
- 1 ounce fresh lime juice
- 1½ teaspoons Simple Syrup (P. 17)
- 4 drops of orange-flower water
- 1 orange twist

Fill a cocktail shaker with ice. Add all of the ingredients except the orange twist and shake vigorously. Strain into a chilled martini glass and garnish with the orange twist.

Pegu

Mixologist and co-owner Audrey Saunders recommends high-proof (94.6 instead of 80) Tanqueray gin in this cocktail buff's favorite.

Pegu Club • New York City

Ice
2 ounces gin
¾ ounce orange curaçao
¾ ounce fresh lime juice
Dash of Angostura bitters
1 lime twist

Fill a cocktail shaker with ice. Add all of the ingredients except the lime twist and shake well. Strain into a chilled martini glass and garnish with the lime twist.

Aviator

Lightly sweetened with maraschino liqueur, Frasca's version of the elegant but often overlooked 1930s cocktail Aviation is one of the restaurant's most popular drinks.

Frasca • Boulder

Ice
2 ounces gin
1 ounce maraschino liqueur
1½ teaspoons fresh lemon juice
1 lemon twist

Fill a cocktail shaker with ice. Add the gin, maraschino liqueur and lemon juice and shake well. Strain into a chilled martini glass and garnish with the lemon twist.

LUCQUES JASMINE
Lucques, Los Angeles

Lucques Jasmine

Lucques • Los Angeles

The popular three-course Sunday suppers prepared by Suzanne Goin (an F&W Best New Chef 1999) are accompanied by themed cocktails.

Ice
- 1 ounce gin
- 2 teaspoons fresh lemon juice
- 1½ teaspoons triple sec
- 1½ teaspoons Simple Syrup (P. 17)
- 1½ teaspoons Campari

Fill a cocktail shaker with ice. Add all of the ingredients, shake well and strain into a chilled martini glass.

Green Light

Tusk Lounge • Baltimore

Two vintage Waterford crystal chandeliers and a 30-foot-long marble bar, built in the late 1800s for a private men's club in Alabama, adorn this lounge at the Brass Elephant restaurant.

Ice
- 3 ounces gin
- 3 ounces triple sec
- 1 ounce fresh lime juice
- 1 lime wheel

Fill a cocktail shaker with ice. Add the gin, triple sec and lime juice and shake well. Strain into a large chilled martini glass and garnish with the lime wheel.

LEMONGRASS MARGARITA, P. 95
Saba Blue Water Cafe, Austin

TEQUILA

Paloma

Jimmy's • Aspen

Known for its tequila cocktails, Jimmy's also serves a tequila key lime pie topped with a splash of silver tequila.

Ice
- 3 ounces fresh grapefruit juice
- 2 ounces reposado tequila
- ½ ounce fresh lime juice
- 1 ounce chilled club soda
- 1 ounce chilled Sprite
- 1 lime wedge

Fill a cocktail shaker with ice. Add the grapefruit juice, reposado tequila and lime juice and shake well. Strain into an ice-filled highball glass, top with the club soda and Sprite and garnish with the lime wedge.

Margarita

Tommy's Mexican Restaurant • San Francisco

Co-owner Julio Bermejo makes his margaritas with neutrally flavored agave nectar—a natural honey-like sweetener from the same plant as tequila—in place of triple sec. It's available at natural food stores and online.

- 1 lime wedge and kosher salt

Ice
- 2 ounces reposado tequila
- 1 ounce fresh lime juice
- ½ ounce agave nectar or juice

Moisten the outer rim of a rocks glass with the lime wedge and coat lightly with salt. Fill a cocktail shaker with ice. Add the tequila, lime juice and agave nectar, shake well and strain into the rocks glass.

Strawberry-Almond Margarita

El Carmen • Los Angeles

This Mexican-themed bar, which is decorated with bull heads, paintings of Mexican wrestlers and wrestling masks, pours over 300 different tequilas.

- 1 cup crushed ice
- 2 ounces silver tequila
- ½ ounce triple sec
- ½ ounce fresh lime juice
- 1½ teaspoons almond syrup
- 3 large strawberries, hulled
- 1 lime wedge

In a blender, combine all of the ingredients except the lime wedge. Blend at high speed until smooth. Pour into a chilled margarita glass and garnish with the lime wedge.

Lemongrass Margarita

Saba Blue Water Cafe • Austin

The bar at this Caribbean-Mexican restaurant is backed by an enormous black-lit aquarium filled with brightly colored tropical fish.

- 1 lime wedge and kosher salt
- Ice
- 1½ ounces gold or reposado tequila
- 1 ounce Lemongrass Syrup (P. 38)
- One 4-inch lemongrass stalk (optional)

Moisten the outer rim of a margarita glass with the lime wedge and coat lightly with salt; reserve the lime. Fill the glass and a cocktail shaker with ice. Add the tequila and syrup to the shaker; shake well. Strain into the glass, top with a squeeze of lime and garnish with the lemongrass, if desired.

PEAR-CILANTRO MARGARITA
De Cero, Chicago

Pear-Cilantro Margarita

De Cero • Chicago

Unusual fruit and herb combinations distinguish the drinks at this upscale taqueria, whose name loosely translates as "from scratch."

Ice
- 1 ounce reposado tequila
- 1 ounce pear nectar or juice
- ½ ounce Simple Syrup (P. 17)
- ½ ounce fresh lime juice
- 1½ teaspoons fresh lemon juice
- ½ teaspoon chopped cilantro, plus 1 small cilantro sprig for garnish

Fill a cocktail shaker with ice. Add all of the ingredients except the cilantro sprig and shake well. Pour into a chilled margarita glass and garnish with the cilantro sprig.

Jula Hoop

Elaine's on Franklin • Chapel Hill, NC

A twist on the cosmopolitan, this drink was created by bartender Julia Hartsell, a professional hula hooper who makes and sells hoops, teaches hula hooping and performs at live events.

Ice
- 2 ounces gold or reposado tequila
- 1 ounce triple sec
- 1 ounce fresh orange juice
- ½ ounce fresh lime juice
- 1½ teaspoons cranberry juice
- 1 orange wheel

Fill a cocktail shaker with ice. Add all of the ingredients except the orange wheel and shake well. Strain into a chilled martini glass and garnish with the orange wheel.

Longhorn Iced Tea

219 West • Austin

This bar's theme nights include Two-Bit Tuesdays, featuring 25-cent corn dogs and two-dollar premium drafts.

Ice
¾ ounce reposado tequila
¾ ounce light rum
¾ ounce vodka
¾ ounce triple sec
2 ounces fresh orange juice
1 ounce fresh lime juice
1 ounce Simple Syrup (P. 17)
1½ teaspoons grenadine
1 lime wheel

Fill a pint glass with ice. Add the tequila, light rum, vodka and triple sec to the pint glass and stir well. Add the fresh orange juice, fresh lime juice and Simple Syrup and stir again. Top the cocktail with the grenadine and garnish with the lime wheel.

El Quijote

Bradley Ogden • Las Vegas

Peach jam, smoky chipotle chile and cinnamon-flavored Goldschläger are the improbably welcome additions to this subtly spicy margarita riff.

Ice
1½ ounces reposado tequila
½ ounce Simple Syrup (P. 17)
½ ounce Grand Marnier
½ ounce fresh lemon juice
1½ teaspoons fresh lime juice
1½ teaspoons Goldschläger
½ teaspoon peach jam
⅛ teaspoon minced canned chipotle chile in adobo
1 lime wheel

Fill a cocktail shaker with ice. Add all of the ingredients except the lime wheel and shake well. Strain into an ice-filled highball glass and garnish with the lime wheel.

Latin Lover

Cibucán • Philadelphia

Cibucán—whose name means "extract" in Taíno, a lost language of the Caribbean—draws on a range of Latin influences for cocktails, as in this combination of pineapple juice, tequila and Brazilian cachaça.

Ice
¾ ounce cachaça
¾ ounce reposado tequila
½ ounce fresh lemon juice
½ ounce fresh lime juice
4 ounces pineapple juice

Fill a cocktail shaker with ice. Add all of the ingredients, shake well and strain into a large chilled martini glass.

LA ROSITA
Zig Zag Café, Seattle

La Rosita

Robert Hess, self-taught bar expert and creator of Drinkboy.com, a Web site for the cocktail-obsessed, introduced this classic to the Zig Zag bartenders.

Zig Zag Café • Seattle

Ice
1½ ounces reposado tequila
½ ounce dry vermouth
½ ounce sweet vermouth
½ ounce Campari

Fill two-thirds of a pint glass with ice. Add all of the ingredients and stir until completely chilled, then strain into a chilled martini glass.

Tequila Blossom

Bar manager Eben Freeman updates a little-known vintage cocktail, the gin-based Grapefruit Blossom, with silver tequila and fresh nasturtiums.

WD-50 • New York City

Ice
2 ounces silver tequila
1½ teaspoons maraschino liqueur
3 ounces fresh grapefruit juice
3 organic nasturtium flowers

Fill a highball glass with ice. Add the tequila and maraschino liqueur, then top with the grapefruit juice. Stir well and garnish with the nasturtium flowers.

MEXICAN THREE-WAY
Chino Latino, Minneapolis

Mexican Three-Way

This restaurant, whose theme is "street food from the hot zones," serves dishes from Mexico, Thailand, Jamaica, Korea and Polynesia—and has late-night dim sum service.

Chino Latino • Minneapolis

1 lime wedge and kosher salt
Ice
3 ounces silver tequila
3 ounces triple sec
1 tablespoon tamarind concentrate
1½ teaspoons fresh lime juice
2 lime wheels

Moisten the outer rim of a pint glass or large highball glass with the lime wedge and coat lightly with salt. Fill the glass and a cocktail shaker with ice. Add the tequila, triple sec, tamarind concentrate and lime juice to the shaker and shake well. Strain into the pint glass and garnish with the lime wheels.

Horny Huck

Dishes at Roaring Fork include Dr Pepper–braised beef short ribs and Colorado beef tenderloin with whiskey "shellac."

Roaring Fork • Scottsdale

1 heaping tablespoon blueberries
Ice
1½ ounces silver tequila
1 ounce lemonade
½ ounce orange curaçao
½ ounce fresh lime juice

In a cocktail shaker, muddle the blueberries. Fill with ice, add the tequila, lemonade, orange curaçao and lime juice and shake well. Strain into a chilled martini glass.

Passion Pulse

I-Bar • Las Vegas

Signature cocktails at this lounge in the center of the Rio Hotel's main casino pit are served by model-waitresses called I-Girls who also perform choreographed dance numbers.

Ice
1 ounce fresh orange juice
1 ounce passion fruit nectar or juice
1 ounce silver tequila
¾ ounce Grand Marnier
½ ounce RémyRed Red Berry Infusion
½ large pasteurized egg white (optional)
Dash of Angostura bitters
Pinch of freshly grated nutmeg

Fill a cocktail shaker with ice. Add all of the ingredients except the nutmeg and shake well. Strain into a chilled martini glass and top with the nutmeg.

El Diablo

Cortez • San Francisco

Whimsical lamps resembling the mobiles that hang over babies' cribs adorn the bar at Pascal Rigo's Mediterranean restaurant in the Hotel Adagio.

Ice
2 ounces silver tequila
½ ounce fresh lime juice
1½ teaspoons crème de cassis
2 ounces chilled ginger beer
1 lime wheel

Fill a highball glass with ice. Add the tequila and lime juice, drizzle with the cassis and top with the ginger beer. Garnish with the lime wheel.

Tuacarita

This twist on the margarita uses Tuaca, a sweet Italian liqueur with distinctive orange and vanilla flavors.

The Whiskey • Houston

Ice
2 ounces silver tequila
1 ounce Tuaca
1½ teaspoons fresh lime juice
1½ teaspoons fresh lemon juice
1½ teaspoons Simple Syrup (P. 17)
1 lime wedge

Fill a cocktail shaker with ice. Add all of the ingredients except the lime wedge and shake well. Strain into a chilled martini glass and garnish with the lime wedge.

Sáicar

This strong but smooth spin on the classic sidecar replaces the traditional Cognac and lemon juice with silver tequila, Mexican brandy and a touch of fresh lime.

Staab House • Santa Fe

1 lime wedge and sugar
Ice
1¼ ounces silver tequila
1¼ ounces brandy
1½ teaspoons triple sec
1 lime wedge and 1 maraschino cherry

Moisten the outer rim of a martini glass with the lime wedge and coat lightly with sugar. Fill a cocktail shaker with ice. Add the tequila, brandy and triple sec and shake well. Strain into the martini glass and garnish with the lime wedge and cherry.

The Devil Inside

This club has four themed lounges (red, orange, blue and bamboo) and Astroturf-covered bathrooms.

Swig • Santa Fe

1 lime wedge and kosher salt
Ice
3 ounces silver tequila
1¼ ounces triple sec
¾ ounce fresh lime juice
1 ounce mezcal

Moisten the outer rim of a large martini glass with the lime wedge and coat lightly with salt. Fill a cocktail shaker with ice. Add the tequila, triple sec and lime juice and shake well. Strain into the martini glass and top with the mezcal.

Melon Mezcalito

This neon-green drink is made with mezcal, a Mexican spirit similar to tequila but with an intensely smoky flavor.

El Farol • Santa Fe

Ice
1 ounce mezcal
½ ounce triple sec
½ ounce Midori
¾ ounce fresh lime juice
1 ounce fresh orange juice
1 lime wheel

Fill a cocktail shaker with ice. Add all of the ingredients except the lime wheel and shake well. Strain into a chilled martini glass and garnish with the lime wheel.

Melon Tequilana

Sushi Samba Dromo • Miami

Noted mixologist Paul Tanguay developed this candy-colored cocktail for the splashy South Beach outpost of this Japanese-Brazilian-Peruvian chain.

- One 3-by-1-inch rectangle of seedless watermelon, plus 1 watermelon triangle for garnish
- ½ teaspoon sugar
- 1½ ounces añejo tequila
- 1 ounce fresh lime juice
- 1½ teaspoons vanilla vodka
- 1½ teaspoons grenadine
- Ice
- 1 to 2 ounces chilled club soda

In a cocktail shaker, muddle the seedless watermelon rectangle with the sugar. Add the añejo tequila, lime juice, vanilla vodka and grenadine and shake well. Strain the drink into an ice-filled highball glass and top with a large splash of chilled club soda. Garnish the cocktail with the watermelon triangle.

FERNANDO'S HIDEAWAY
Schiller's Liquor Bar,
New York City

Batanga

Batanga—Spanish slang for "thick in the middle"—was the nickname of a rotund regular at La Capilla, a renowned bar in Tequila, Mexico, where this drink originated half a century ago.

Diego • Las Vegas

Ice
1½ ounces añejo tequila
1 ounce fresh lime juice
Pinch of salt
2 ounces chilled Coca-Cola
1 lime wedge

Fill a cocktail shaker with ice. Add the tequila, lime juice and salt and shake well. Strain into an ice-filled highball glass, top with the Coca-Cola and garnish with the lime wedge.

Fernando's Hideaway

When Mexican-born employee Fernando Cabrera created this drink, the restaurant's management liked it so much, they gave it a permanent place on the menu.

Schiller's Liquor Bar • New York City

Ice
1¼ ounces añejo tequila
1 ounce peach liqueur
½ ounce peach nectar or juice
½ ounce fresh lime juice
½ ounce fresh orange juice
1 lime wheel

Fill a cocktail shaker with ice. Add all of the ingredients except the lime wheel and shake well. Strain into a chilled martini glass and garnish with the lime wheel.

SOUTHERN CUCUMBER (LEFT), P. 117
Brazen Bean, Portland, OR
LINSTEAD, P. 120
Lilette, New Orleans

WHISKEY

Whiskey Sour

This restaurant in an early-19th-century Harvard theatrical club serves an exceptional (if untraditional) whiskey sour lightly sweetened with fresh orange juice.

UpStairs on the Square • Cambridge, MA

Ice
2 ounces Canadian whisky
¾ ounce fresh lemon juice
½ ounce fresh orange juice
½ ounce Simple Syrup (P. 17)
1 tablespoon pasteurized egg white (optional)
1 orange wheel and 1 maraschino cherry

Fill a cocktail shaker with ice. Add the whisky, citrus juices, Simple Syrup and egg white and shake vigorously. Strain into a rocks glass over ice and garnish with the orange wheel and cherry.

McCrady's Manhattan

McCrady's is Charleston's first tavern, built in 1778 in the heart of the city's historic French Quarter.

McCrady's • Charleston

Ice
1½ ounces Canadian whisky
½ ounce sweet vermouth
1½ teaspoons cherry brandy
½ teaspoon Simple Syrup (P. 17)

Fill a cocktail shaker with ice. Add all of the ingredients, shake well and strain into a chilled martini glass.

Mint Julep

Round Robin Bar • Washington, D.C.

Bartender Jim Hewes has been serving this mint julep, a family recipe from 19th-century Kentucky senator Henry Clay, for 20 years.

- 15 mint leaves, plus 1 mint sprig for garnish
- 1 teaspoon sugar
- 2½ ounces bourbon
- Crushed ice
- 2 ounces chilled club soda
- 1 lemon twist and powdered sugar

In a highball glass, muddle the mint leaves with the sugar and ½ teaspoon of the bourbon. Add a handful of crushed ice and stir gently with a long-handled spoon. Fill the glass with crushed ice, add the remaining bourbon and top with the club soda. Garnish with the lemon twist, mint sprig and a sprinkling of powdered sugar.

Pimlico

The Hungry Cat • Hollywood, CA

"It seems L.A. people only want to drink vodka," says chef-owner David Lentz, who based the Pimlico on a cocktail his grandfather used to drink. "I want them to try bourbon."

- 20 mint leaves, plus 1 mint sprig for garnish
- 1 ounce Simple Syrup (P. 17)
- Ice
- 1½ ounces bourbon
- 1 ounce fresh orange juice
- ¾ ounce fresh lime juice

In a cocktail shaker, muddle the mint leaves with the Simple Syrup. Fill the shaker with ice, add the bourbon, orange juice and lime juice and shake well. Strain into a rocks glass over ice and garnish with the mint sprig.

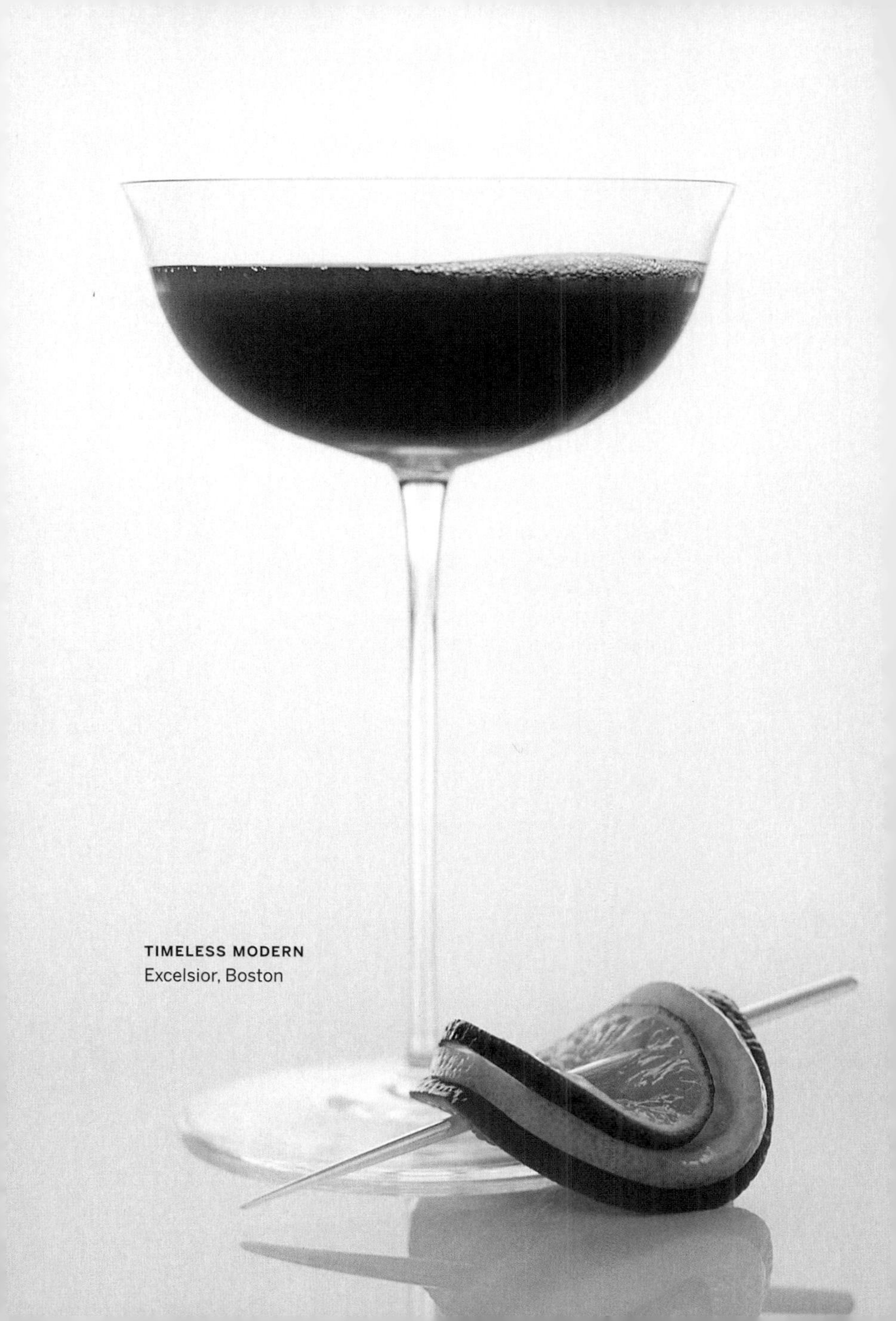

TIMELESS MODERN
Excelsior, Boston

Timeless Modern

Excelsior's glass elevator ascends through a three-story wine tower that separates the bar from the dining room.

Excelsior • Boston

- 2 thin lemon wheels
- 2 thin lime wheels
- 3 thin orange wheels
- 1½ teaspoons maraschino liqueur
- ½ teaspoon grenadine
- Dash of Angostura bitters
- 1 maraschino cherry
- 2½ ounces bourbon
- Ice

Set aside 1 wheel of each citrus fruit. In a cocktail shaker, muddle all of the ingredients except the bourbon and ice. Add the bourbon and ice and shake well. Strain into a chilled martini glass and garnish with the reserved citrus wheels.

Perfect Mark

The bartenders experimented with Americanos (Campari and sweet vermouth) and Manhattans (bourbon and sweet vermouth) until they arrived at this inspired combination (Maker's Mark, Campari and sweet vermouth).

Inman Park Patio • Atlanta

- Ice
- 2 ounces bourbon
- ¾ ounce sweet vermouth
- ½ ounce Campari
- 1 maraschino cherry

Fill a cocktail shaker with ice. Add the bourbon, sweet vermouth and Campari and shake well. Strain into a chilled martini glass and garnish with the cherry.

Old-Fashioned

Park Place on Main • Louisville

General manager and resident bourbon expert Jerry Slater adds a splash of fresh lemon juice and simple syrup to his version of this 19th-century cocktail, said to have originated at Louisville's members-only Pendennis Club.

- 2 sugar cubes
- 1 orange wheel
- 1 maraschino cherry
- 2 dashes of Angostura bitters
- Ice
- 2 ounces bourbon
- 1½ teaspoons fresh lemon juice
- 1½ teaspoons Simple Syrup (P. 17)
- ½ to 1 ounce chilled club soda

In a rocks glass, muddle the sugar cubes with the orange wheel, cherry and bitters until the sugar is completely dissolved. Discard the orange wheel. Fill the glass with ice. Add the bourbon, lemon juice and Simple Syrup, then top with the chilled club soda.

Marked Car

2527 • Cleveland

Occupying a former motorcycle repair shop, this upscale bar tweaks the traditional sidecar by replacing brandy with Maker's Mark bourbon.

- Ice
- 3 ounces bourbon
- ½ ounce triple sec
- ½ ounce fresh lemon juice
- ½ ounce Simple Syrup (P. 17)
- 1 maraschino cherry

Fill a cocktail shaker with ice. Add all of the ingredients except the cherry and shake well. Strain into a chilled martini glass and garnish with the cherry.

Southern Cucumber

Co-owner Huston Davis believes muddled cucumber gives this drink a refreshing quality reminiscent of fresh-squeezed lemonade.

Brazen Bean • Portland, OR

- ½ cup diced seedless cucumber, plus 1 cucumber spear for garnish
- ½ ounce Simple Syrup (P. 17)
- 2 ounces bourbon
- ½ ounce fresh lemon juice
- ½ ounce fresh lime juice
- Ice
- 2 ounces chilled ginger ale

In a cocktail shaker, lightly muddle the diced cucumber with the Simple Syrup. Add the bourbon, lemon juice, lime juice and enough ice to fill a highball glass; shake well. Pour into a highball glass, top with the ginger ale and garnish with the cucumber spear.

Nutty Kentucky

This modern American restaurant in the new Mandarin Oriental Hotel boasts D.C.'s largest selection of single-malt whiskeys.

CityZen • Washington, D.C.

- Ice
- 2½ ounces bourbon
- 1½ ounces Frangelico
- ½ ounce fresh lemon juice
- 1 lemon wedge and 1 lemon twist

Fill a cocktail shaker with ice. Add the bourbon, Frangelico and lemon juice and shake well. Strain into a chilled martini glass, top with a squeeze of lemon and garnish with the lemon twist.

STILETTO
Cosmos, Minneapolis

Stiletto

Cosmos • Minneapolis

Brandy-soaked cherries and small-batch Knob Creek bourbon distinguish this almond-tinged whiskey sour served in the restaurant and lounge of Le Meridien hotel.

Ice
1½ ounces bourbon
½ ounce amaretto
½ ounce fresh lemon juice
1 or 2 brandied or maraschino cherries

Fill a cocktail shaker with ice. Add the bourbon, amaretto and lemon juice and shake well. Strain into a rocks glass over ice and garnish with the cherry or cherries.

The Southerner

Harrison • Portland, OR

Cigar aficionados can visit the restaurant's Blue Room, where a custom ventilation system purifies the air every 90 seconds.

Ice
1½ ounces bourbon
½ large pasteurized egg white (optional)
¾ ounce Simple Syrup (P. 17)
¾ ounce fresh lemon juice
½ ounce fresh orange juice
1 very small pinch of ground cloves
Dash of Angostura bitters
1 large orange twist

Fill a cocktail shaker with ice. Add all of the ingredients except the orange twist and shake well, then strain into a chilled martini glass. Flame the orange twist over the drink (P. 16) and drop it in.

Linstead

Lilette • New Orleans

Nearly all of the drinks on Lilette's cocktail menu are originals. Linstead is the work of retired bartender Eric Palmer, who is so missed that the restaurant's managers are thinking of renaming the drink The Palmer.

- Ice
- 1½ ounces bourbon
- ½ ounce pineapple juice
- 1½ teaspoons Pernod
- ½ teaspoon fresh lemon juice
- ½ teaspoon fresh lime juice
- 1 maraschino cherry

Fill a cocktail shaker with ice. Add all of the ingredients except the cherry and shake well. Strain into a chilled martini glass and garnish with the cherry.

Lincoln's Honeysuckle Rose

Limestone • Louisville

This restaurant is named for the limestone traces found in Kentucky springwater, thought to be a crucial ingredient in the state's famous whiskey.

- Ice
- 1½ ounces bourbon
- 1 teaspoon honey
- ½ ounce Tuaca
- 1 to 1½ teaspoons rose water
- 1 lemon twist

Fill a cocktail shaker with ice. Add all of the ingredients except the lemon twist and shake well. Strain into a small rocks glass over ice and garnish with the lemon twist.

Louisville Lemonade

Avalon • Louisville

Avalon's most popular drink was created as a summer refresher, but customer demand has kept it on the menu year-round.

Ice
2 ounces frozen lemonade concentrate
1½ ounces bourbon
1½ ounces Southern Comfort
½ ounce fresh orange juice
1½ teaspoons triple sec
1 lemon wheel and 1 orange wheel

Fill a cocktail shaker with ice. Add all of the ingredients except the citrus wheels and shake well. Strain into a highball glass over ice and garnish with the citrus wheels.

Manhattan

Star Lounge • New York City

Norman Bukofzer, renowned bartender at the Ritz-Carlton Central Park's Star Lounge prefers to garnish his Manhattan with a simple orange twist. "Nice and elegant," he says. "This is the Ritz."

Ice
2½ ounces bourbon or rye
1 ounce sweet vermouth
2 dashes of Angostura or orange bitters
1 orange twist

Fill two-thirds of a pint glass or cocktail shaker with ice. Add the bourbon, sweet vermouth and bitters and let stand for 15 seconds, then stir 15 times to chill. Strain into a chilled martini glass and garnish with the orange twist.

WRY MANHATTAN
Cowboy Ciao, Scottsdale

Algonquin

Pin-Up Bowl • St. Louis

This quirky bowling alley and cocktail lounge serves old-school drinks and snacks like Campbell's tomato soup and Pop Tarts.

Ice
2 ounces rye
1 ounce dry vermouth
1 ounce pineapple juice
1 maraschino cherry or orange twist

Fill a cocktail shaker with ice. Add the rye, vermouth and pineapple juice and shake well. Strain into a chilled martini glass and garnish with the cherry or orange twist.

Wry Manhattan

Cowboy Ciao • Scottsdale

The Wry Manhattan was created to honor Fritz Maytag, the San Francisco brewer and distiller behind Anchor Steam beer and Old Potrero single-malt rye whiskey.

Ice
1½ ounces rye
1 ounce Southern Comfort
1½ teaspoons grenadine
Dash of Angostura bitters
2 dried sweet cherries on a pick

Fill a cocktail shaker with ice. Add the rye, Southern Comfort, grenadine and bitters and shake well. Strain into a chilled martini glass and garnish with the dried cherries.

Sazerac

The Library Lounge • New Orleans

Made from a 200-year-old recipe, aromatic, herb-flavored Peychaud's bitters are available by mail order (sazerac.com). "It just wouldn't be a Sazerac without Peychaud's," says bartender Chris McMillian.

Splash of Pernod
1 or 2 sugar cubes
2 or 3 dashes of Peychaud's bitters
2 or 3 dashes of Angostura bitters
Small splash of chilled club soda
2 ounces rye
Ice
1 lemon twist

Rinse a chilled rocks glass with the Pernod. In another rocks glass, muddle the sugar cubes with the bitters and club soda until the sugar is completely dissolved. Add the rye, fill the glass with ice and stir until completely chilled. Strain into the Pernod-rinsed glass and garnish with the lemon twist.

Deshler

Zig Zag Cafe • Seattle

Head bartender Murray Stenson draws a loyal crowd for little-known cocktails like the Deshler, which combines rye, the oldest American whiskey, and Dubonnet, a wine-based aperitif similar to vermouth.

Ice
¾ ounce rye
¾ ounce Dubonnet Rouge
½ ounce triple sec
2 dashes of Angostura bitters

Fill two-thirds of a pint glass or cocktail shaker with ice. Add all of the ingredients and stir until completely chilled, then strain into a chilled martini glass.

Artist's Special

Forest Room 5 • Denver

This lounge, café and art gallery occupies a 19th-century fire station known as Tabor Hose House 5, which abuts the former Forest Street.

Ice
1 ounce scotch
1 ounce sweet sherry
½ ounce fresh lemon juice
1½ teaspoons grenadine

Fill a cocktail shaker with ice. Add all of the ingredients, shake well and strain into a chilled martini glass.

Scotty & Tammy

Taj • New York City

Beverage consultant Jerri Banks developed the tea-based Scotty & Tammy to complement Taj's Indian-inspired food. She prefers using the brand In Pursuit of Tea for the intense bergamot flavor of its Earl Grey.

Ice
2 ounces blended scotch
1½ ounces fresh lemon juice
¾ ounce tamarind syrup
¾ ounce chilled Earl Grey tea
1 lemon wedge

Fill a cocktail shaker with ice. Add all of the ingredients except the lemon wedge and shake well. Strain into a rocks glass over ice and top with a squeeze of lemon.

SMOKY APPLE
Mistral, Boston

Smoky Apple

Mistral • Boston

Not to be confused with the candy-sweet apple martini, this cocktail combines rich blended scotch with apple schnapps and spicy Angostura bitters.

Ice
2 ounces blended scotch
1½ ounces apple schnapps
Dash of Angostura bitters
1 thin slice of Granny Smith apple

Fill two-thirds of a pint glass with ice. Add the scotch, apple schnapps and bitters and stir until completely chilled. Strain into a chilled martini glass and garnish with the apple slice.

Mystique

The Drálion • Dallas

Used Mercedes dealer–turned–restaurateur Khanh Dao developed this unlikely blend of smoky scotch, honey-flavored Drambuie and sweet fruit liqueurs.

Ice
1 ounce blended scotch
½ ounce Drambuie
1½ teaspoons maraschino liqueur
½ teaspoon peach schnapps
1 orange twist and 1 maraschino cherry

Fill two-thirds of a pint glass or cocktail shaker with ice. Add the scotch, Drambuie, maraschino liqueur and schnapps and stir until completely chilled. Strain into a highball glass over ice and garnish with the orange twist and cherry.

SUMO IN A SIDECAR (LEFT), P. 138
Buddakan, Philadelphia
GAMMA RAY, P. 139
5 Ninth, New York City

BRANDY

Pisco Sour

A Prohibition-era favorite, this drink uses pisco, a South American brandy made from Muscat grapes and aged in large clay jars.

Bemelmans Bar • New York City

Ice
1½ ounces pisco brandy
1 ounce Simple Syrup (P. 17)
¾ ounce fresh lemon juice
1 large pasteurized egg white
3 or 4 drops of Angostura bitters

Fill a cocktail shaker with ice. Add all of the ingredients except the bitters and shake vigorously. Strain into a chilled martini glass and top with the bitters.

Sidecar

Fans of Milk & Honey, a Lower East Side speakeasy known for its strict house rules and peerless cocktails, can find the same drinks, plus an oyster bar, at owner Sasha Petraske's latest venture.

Little Branch • New York City

Ice
1½ ounces Cognac, preferably Pierre Ferrand
1 ounce triple sec, preferably Cointreau
½ ounce fresh lemon juice

Fill a cocktail shaker with ice. Add all of the ingredients, shake well and strain into a chilled martini glass.

Party Hardly

Beauty Shop • Memphis

Food and cocktails are served at refurbished hair dryer stations in this beauty parlor–turned–lounge and restaurant.

Ice
2 ounces Cognac
1 ounce pineapple juice
½ ounce chilled ginger ale
Dash of Angostura bitters

Fill a cocktail shaker with ice. Add all of the ingredients, shake well and strain into a chilled martini glass.

French 75

The Velvet Tango Room • Cleveland

Metal shutters often obscure the sign at Cleveland's most discreet cocktail lounge.

Ice
2 ounces Cognac
½ ounce fresh lemon juice
1½ teaspoons Simple Syrup (P. 17)
2 ounces chilled Champagne
1 lemon twist

Fill a cocktail shaker with ice. Add the Cognac, lemon juice and Simple Syrup and shake well. Strain into a chilled martini glass, top with the Champagne and garnish with the lemon twist.

THE JADE
Zola, Washington, D.C.

Via Veneto

Shake this drink vigorously to emulsify the egg white for a frothy consistency.

Pace • New York City

Ice
2 ounces Cognac
1 ounce fresh lemon juice
½ ounce Simple Syrup (P. 17)
½ large pasteurized egg white (optional)
Dash of sambuca
1 lemon twist

Fill a cocktail shaker with ice. Add all of the ingredients except the lemon twist and shake well. Strain into a chilled martini glass and garnish with the lemon twist.

The Jade

Zola continues the theme of the adjoining International Spy Museum with design touches like a hidden revolving door that leads to the bathrooms.

Zola • Washington, D.C.

1 lime wedge and kosher salt
Ice
2 ounces grappa
½ ounce Grand Marnier
½ ounce fresh lemon juice
½ ounce fresh lime juice
½ ounce Simple Syrup (P. 17)
½ teaspoon blue curaçao
1 lime wheel

Moisten the outer rim of a martini glass with the lime wedge and coat with salt. Fill a cocktail shaker with ice. Add all of the remaining ingredients except the curaçao and lime wheel and shake well. Strain into the martini glass, add the curaçao and garnish with the lime wheel.

Focoso

Arcodoro & Pomodoro • Dallas

At Arcodoro & Pomodoro, *grappa di fragola*, a strawberry-infused grappa, replaces the muddled strawberry and unflavored grappa that are called for here.

- 1 strawberry
- 1 ounce grappa
- ½ ounce dry vermouth
- 2 drops of grenadine
- Ice
- 3 ounces chilled prosecco

In a cocktail shaker, lightly muddle the strawberry. Add the grappa, dry vermouth, grenadine and ice and shake well. Strain into a chilled flute and top with the prosecco.

McIntosh Cocktail

Mediterraneo • Providence

This drink combines the all-American flavors of apple and cranberry. Applejack is a native brandy that dates to the late 1600s.

- Ice
- 1¼ ounces applejack brandy
- ½ ounce Chambord
- 2 ounces cranberry juice

Fill a cocktail shaker with ice. Add all of the ingredients, shake well and strain into a rocks glass over ice.

Big Apple Manhattan

Little Giant • New York City

This drink was the "apple pie" for Little Giant's liquid Thanksgiving. The "turkey" was a mint julep made with Wild Turkey.

Ice
2 ounces applejack brandy
½ ounce sweet vermouth
1 ounce apple cider
Dash of Angostura bitters

Fill a cocktail shaker with ice. Add all of the ingredients, shake well and strain into a chilled martini glass.

Caffè Notte

Brasa • Seattle

Shaking this cocktail creates a layer of foam on top, like the *crema* on an espresso. *Notte,* Italian for "night," refers both to the drink's dark color and to the time you'd drink it.

Ice
1 ounce Calvados
1 ounce coffee liqueur, preferably Tia Maria
½ ounce room-temperature brewed espresso

Fill a cocktail shaker with ice. Add all of the ingredients, shake vigorously and strain into a chilled martini glass.

PEAR BRANDY KAMI KAZI
Paley's Place, Portland, OR

Apple Sour

This café and bar offers more than 500 spirits and fortified wines. The Apple Sour can be made with any of 13 different bottlings of Calvados.

César • Berkeley, CA

Ice
1½ ounces Calvados
¾ ounce fresh lemon juice
1 teaspoon pure maple syrup
1 maraschino cherry

Fill a cocktail shaker with ice. Add the Calvados, lemon juice and maple syrup and shake well. Strain into a chilled martini glass and garnish with the cherry.

Pear Brandy Kami Kazi

Chef and owner (and avid cyclist) Vitaly Paley recently developed the Paleybar, an all-natural energy bar that he sells at the restaurant.

Paley's Place • Portland, OR

Ice
2 ounces pear eau-de-vie
1 ounce triple sec
¾ ounce fresh lime juice
1½ teaspoons Simple Syrup (P. 17)
1 lime wheel

Fill a cocktail shaker with ice. Add all of the ingredients except the lime wheel and shake well. Strain into a chilled martini glass and garnish with the lime wheel.

Falling Leaves

Pegu Club • New York City

At the Pegu Club, this drink is made with intensely aromatic Clear Creek pear eau-de-vie from Oregon; each 750-ml bottle is distilled from nearly 30 pounds of fresh fruit.

- 1 teaspoon honey
- ½ teaspoon water
- 2¼ ounces dry Riesling
- 1 ounce pear eau-de-vie
- 1½ teaspoons orange curaçao, preferably Marie Brizard
- Ice
- 1 whole star anise

In a cocktail shaker, stir together the honey and water. Add the Riesling, eau-de-vie and curaçao, fill with ice and shake well. Strain into a chilled martini glass and garnish with the star anise.

Sumo in a Sidecar

Buddakan • Philadelphia

Buddakan makes its version of the sidecar with apricot brandy in place of the traditional Cognac and then adds sake for an Asian twist.

- 1 lime wedge and sugar
- Ice
- 1¾ ounces apricot brandy
- 1¾ ounces sake
- ½ ounce fresh lemon juice
- 1½ teaspoons Simple Syrup (P. 17)
- 1 dried apricot

Moisten the outer rim of a martini glass with the lemon wedge and coat with sugar. Fill a cocktail shaker with ice. Add all of the remaining ingredients except the dried apricot and shake well. Strain into the martini glass and garnish with the apricot.

The 23

This robust combination of Armagnac, sweet vermouth and lemon juice is an elegant alternative to the typical steak-house gin martini.

Grill 23 & Bar • Boston

1 lemon wedge and sugar
Ice
2½ ounces Armagnac
½ ounce sweet vermouth
½ ounce fresh lemon juice
2 dashes of Angostura bitters
1 lemon twist

Moisten the outer rim of a martini glass with the lime wedge and coat with sugar. Fill a cocktail shaker with ice. Add all of the remaining ingredients except the lemon twist and shake well. Strain into the martini glass and garnish with the lemon twist.

Gamma Ray

Bartenders at 5 Ninth sprinkle this potent spin on a stinger with cayenne pepper and serve it with a small glass of ice water.

5 Ninth • New York City

Ice
2¼ ounces VSOP Armagnac
¾ ounce white crème de menthe
1 large lemon twist and cayenne pepper

Fill two-thirds of a pint glass with ice. Add the Armagnac and crème de menthe and gently stir until thoroughly chilled. Strain into a chilled martini glass. Flame the lemon twist over the drink (P. 16), drop it in and sprinkle with cayenne pepper.

LUCKY BAMBOO, P. 145
Bambuddha Lounge,
San Francisco

LIQUEUR & VERMOUTH

Negroni

This drink was allegedly born in Italy in the 1920s, when Count Camillo Negroni requested a stronger version of the Americano made with gin in place of club soda.

Nizza La Bella • Albany, CA

Ice
1 ounce gin
1 ounce Campari
1 ounce sweet vermouth
1 large lemon twist

Fill two-thirds of a pint glass with ice. Add the gin, Campari and sweet vermouth and stir until chilled. Strain into a chilled martini glass. Flame the lemon twist over the drink (P. 16) and drop it in.

French Martini

Fresh lemon juice and Champagne balance the sweetness in The Davenport's version of a drink originally made with vodka, Chambord and pineapple juice.

The Davenport • Houston

Ice
1½ ounces Grand Marnier
¾ ounce Chambord
½ ounce fresh lemon juice
2 ounces Champagne

Fill a cocktail shaker with ice. Add the Grand Marnier, Chambord and lemon juice and shake well. Strain into a chilled martini glass and top with the Champagne.

Tiger's Milk

The orange-wheel garnish and coconut milk in this unusual creamy cocktail suggest tiger stripes.

Zoë Pan-Asian Café • St. Louis

Ice
1½ ounces Grand Marnier
1½ ounces fresh orange juice
1½ ounces pineapple juice
½ ounce unsweetened coconut milk from a well-shaken can
1 orange wheel

Fill a cocktail shaker with ice. Add all of the ingredients except the orange wheel and shake well. Strain into a chilled martini glass and garnish with the orange wheel.

Chop Chop Rouge

The 65-foot-long pewter and zinc bar at this Vegas outpost of Thomas Keller's Napa Valley bistro was custom-made in Lyon and shipped to the U.S. in three pieces.

Bouchon • Las Vegas

Ice
1 ounce Grand Marnier
1 ounce RémyRed
½ ounce passion fruit nectar or juice
½ ounce fresh orange juice
1 long orange twist

Fill a cocktail shaker with ice. Add all of the ingredients except the orange twist and shake well. Strain into a chilled martini glass and garnish with the orange twist.

Attorneytini

This bar's cocktail list is called the Martini Hall of Fame, with drinks named for Cleveland "movers and shakers." The Attorneytini honors Jakki and Fred Nance, local lawyers.

Century • Cleveland

- 1 lime wedge
- 2 tablespoons blanched almonds, finely crushed
- Ice
- ½ ounce amaretto
- ½ ounce Southern Comfort
- ½ ounce vodka
- ½ teaspoon Midori
- ½ ounce cranberry juice

Moisten the outer rim of a martini glass with the lime wedge and coat with the crushed almonds. Fill a cocktail shaker with ice. Add all of the remaining ingredients, shake well and strain into the martini glass.

Pink Panther

Owner Jim Russell named this pink drink, a limoncello-spiked twist on the sea breeze, for the 1963 film starring his favorite actor, the late Peter Sellers.

Delmar Restaurant & Lounge • St. Louis

- Ice
- 1 ounce limoncello
- 1 ounce lemon vodka
- ½ ounce fresh red grapefruit juice
- ½ ounce cranberry juice
- 1 lemon twist

Fill a cocktail shaker with ice. Add all of the ingredients except the lemon twist and shake well. Strain into a chilled martini glass and garnish with the lemon twist.

Lucky Bamboo

Bambuddha Lounge • San Francisco

An enormous Buddha reclines on the roof of this lounge in the Phoenix Hotel, a refurbished 1950s motor lodge.

Ice
2½ ounces Pimm's No. 1 Cup
1 ounce Ginger Syrup (below)
3 ounces chilled ginger beer
1 lime wedge and 1 thin strip of cucumber

In an ice-filled highball glass, combine the Pimm's, Ginger Syrup and ginger beer. Add a squeeze of lime; garnish with the cucumber.

GINGER SYRUP In a small saucepan, combine ½ cup of freshly grated ginger with ½ cup of sugar and 1½ cups of water. Bring to a boil, then simmer over low heat until reduced to about 1¼ cups. Strain, let cool and refrigerate for up to 5 days. Makes 10 ounces of syrup.

London Mojito

The Terrace • Seattle

In place of the rum in a traditional mojito, this cocktail by locally renowned bartender Michael Vezzoni uses gin and Pimm's No. 1 Cup, a gin-based herbal aperitif.

8 mint leaves, plus 1 mint sprig for garnish
½ ounce Simple Syrup (P. 17)
2 ounces fresh lime juice
1 ounce Pimm's No. 1 Cup
½ ounce gin
Ice
1 to 2 ounces chilled club soda

In a cocktail shaker, muddle the mint leaves with the Simple Syrup. Add the lime juice, Pimm's, gin and ice and shake well. Strain into an ice-filled highball glass, top with the club soda and garnish with the mint sprig.

HARBOR BREEZE
Pavilion Bar,
Charleston

Harbor Breeze

This rooftop bar at the Market Pavilion Hotel offers a panoramic view of Charleston Harbor, the Cooper River Bridge and, in the distance, historic Fort Sumter.

Pavilion Bar • Charleston

Ice
1½ ounces Midori
½ ounce triple sec
2 ounces fresh orange juice
1 ounce fresh lemon juice
1 ounce fresh lime juice
1 ounce Simple Syrup (P. 17)
1 ounce pineapple juice

In an ice-filled pint glass, combine the Midori and triple sec, then add all of the remaining ingredients and stir.

Jungle Fever

Manager Kate Bocson created Jungle Fever to use up a shipment of mango liqueur that was mistakenly delivered to the lounge. Her garnish: a vodka-soaked pineapple ring.

Cinq • Royal Oak, MI

Ice
½ ounce coconut rum
½ ounce mango liqueur
½ ounce Midori
½ ounce pineapple juice
1½ teaspoons crème de banane

Fill a cocktail shaker with ice. Add all of the ingredients, shake well and strain into a chilled martini glass.

Swamp Gas

Cobalt • New Orleans

Cobalt mixes this tart cocktail with locally distilled, superpremium Cane Louisiana Rum and Hpnotiq, a blue-tinted liqueur made with vodka, tropical fruit juices and Cognac.

Ice
1 ounce light rum
¾ ounce triple sec
½ ounce Hpnotiq
½ ounce fresh lime juice
1 lime twist

Fill a cocktail shaker with ice. Add all of the ingredients except the lime twist and shake well. Strain into a chilled martini glass and garnish with the lime twist.

Soda de Crema

Modesto • St. Louis

Sweet, vanilla-flavored Licor 43 is a widely available Spanish liqueur infused with herbs, citrus fruits and spices—43 ingredients in all.

Ice
1½ ounces Licor 43
4 ounces chilled club soda
1 lime wedge

Fill a highball glass with ice. Add the Licor 43, top with the club soda and a squeeze of lime and stir well.

Ouzorita

Zaytinya • Washington, D.C.

Zaytinya makes its margarita with Hangar One Kaffir Lime vodka (in place of the unflavored vodka and kaffir lime leaf used here) and pungent, anise-flavored Greek ouzo.

- 1 lime wedge and kosher salt
- Ice
- 1½ ounces vodka
- ½ ounce ouzo
- ½ ounce triple sec
- 1 ounce fresh lime juice
- 1 kaffir lime leaf

Moisten the outer rim of a martini glass with the lime wedge and coat lightly with salt. Fill a cocktail shaker with ice. Add all of the remaining ingredients, shake well and strain into the martini glass.

Agavero Punch

Mirepoix • Denver

Agavero is a liqueur made from a blend of tequilas—reposado and añejo—and essence of damiana, a flower native to the mountains of Mexico's tequila-producing Jalisco region.

- Ice
- 2 ounces Agavero tequila liqueur
- ½ ounce Chambord
- 3 to 4 ounces pineapple juice
- 1 lime wedge

Fill a rocks glass with ice. Add the Agavero liqueur and Chambord, top with the pineapple juice and a squeeze of lime and stir well.

SAVONAROLA
Hearth,
New York City

Half Sinner, Half Saint

The restaurant prepares this bracing aperitif with Herbsaint, an anise-flavored spirit made by the New Orleans–based company Sazerac.

Herbsaint • New Orleans

Crushed ice
2 ounces sweet vermouth
2 ounces dry vermouth
½ teaspoon Herbsaint or Pernod
1 lemon twist

Fill a rocks glass with crushed ice. Add the sweet vermouth, dry vermouth and Herbsaint and stir well. Garnish with the lemon twist.

Savonarola

This drink is named for a 15th-century Italian monk who was hanged for preaching against the excesses of Renaissance life. It's made with Italian vermouth and Frangelico, which comes in a bottle shaped like a monk.

Hearth • New York City

Ice
1½ ounces sweet vermouth
½ ounce Frangelico
1 ounce fresh lemon juice
1 ounce fresh lime juice
1 ounce Simple Syrup (P. 17)
1 orange wedge and 1 maraschino cherry

In an ice-filled rocks glass, combine the sweet vermouth and Frangelico. Add the lemon juice, lime juice and Simple Syrup and stir well. Garnish with the orange wedge and cherry.

LEMON SORBET MARTINI (LEFT), P. 164
The Bosco, Ferndale, MI
LEMONTONIA, P. 164
Blue Gin, Washington, D.C.

DESSERT DRINKS

153

Espresso Martini

High Cotton • Charleston

High Cotton, which serves roughly 800 Espresso Martinis a month, takes its name from an old southern term for living well; high-growing cotton was a sign of prosperity.

- 1 small orange wedge and unsweetened cocoa powder
- Ice
- 1 ounce coffee liqueur
- 1 ounce vodka
- 1 ounce room-temperature brewed espresso

Moisten the outer rim of a martini glass with the orange wedge and coat lightly with cocoa powder. Fill a cocktail shaker with ice. Add all of the remaining ingredients, shake well and strain into the martini glass.

Huber's Iced Spanish Coffee

Huber's • Portland, OR

When Huber's, Portland's oldest restaurant, opened as a saloon in 1879, its cocktails came with a complimentary turkey sandwich.

- ¾ ounce overproof rum
- 1½ teaspoons triple sec
- 1½ ounces coffee liqueur, preferably Kahlúa
- Ice
- 4 ounces cold strong coffee
- ¼ cup unsweetened whipped cream and freshly grated nutmeg

In a small saucepan, combine the rum and triple sec and ignite with a long match. Carefully add the coffee liqueur, then pour the flaming mixture into an ice-filled pint glass. Add the coffee, top with the whipped cream and garnish with a sprinkle of freshly grated nutmeg.

Decadence

Tabla • New York City

Bartender Jeff Hansen devised this elegant pick-me-up, which plays on the classic combination of espresso and orange but is served chilled.

Ice
1½ ounces vodka
½ ounce Grand Marnier
¾ ounce room-temperature brewed espresso
1 orange twist

Fill a cocktail shaker with ice. Add the vodka, Grand Marnier and espresso and shake well. Strain into a chilled martini glass and garnish with the orange twist

Café Ferré

Ferré • Dallas

A rim of finely crushed hazelnuts garnishes this Italian restaurant's signature after-dinner drink.

1 orange wedge and 2 tablespoons finely crushed, toasted hazelnuts
1 ounce Irish cream liqueur
1 ounce Tuaca
1 ounce Frangelico
12 ounces hot strong coffee
2 tablespoons unsweetened whipped cream, ground cinnamon and 1 mint sprig

Moisten the outer rim of a large mug or heatproof glass with the orange wedge and coat lightly with the crushed hazelnuts. Add the cream liqueur, Tuaca and Frangelico and top with the coffee. Garnish with the whipped cream, a sprinkle of cinnamon and the mint sprig.

CHOCOLATE RUSSIAN MOJITO
The Abbey,
West Hollywood, CA

Chocolate Russian Mojito

The Abbey • West Hollywood, CA

This sprawling club (there are four bars in all) hosts an annual Academy Awards party whose total proceeds are donated to AIDS Project L.A. Last year's party raised more than $400,000.

¼ lime, cut into 2 pieces
1½ ounces Simple Syrup (P. 17)
4 mint sprigs
Ice
2½ to 3 ounces chocolate vodka
½ ounce dark rum, preferably Gosling's

In a pint glass or cocktail shaker, muddle the lime pieces with the Simple Syrup and 3 of the mint sprigs, then strain into an ice-filled highball glass. Add the vodka, top with the rum and garnish with the remaining mint sprig.

Evil Twin Martini

The Oakroom • Louisville

"Evil twin" was bartender Janet South's nickname for Godiva white-chocolate liqueur, the lesser-known sibling of Godiva dark-chocolate liqueur.

Ice
½ ounce vodka
½ ounce white-chocolate liqueur
½ ounce dark-chocolate liqueur
½ ounce Chambord
1 raspberry

Fill a cocktail shaker with ice. Add all of the ingredients except the raspberry and shake well. Strain into a chilled martini glass and garnish with the raspberry.

S'moretini

S'moretini is the adult version of the beloved kids' treat. Be sure to use a martini glass that can stand up to hot coffee.

Silver Cloud • Chicago

- 2 tablespoons chocolate syrup and finely crushed graham crackers
- ¾ ounce vodka
- ¾ ounce dark-chocolate liqueur
- ¾ ounce crème de cacao
- 4 ounces hot strong coffee
- 2 tablespoons unsweetened whipped cream, 1 toasted marshmallow and chocolate shavings

Coat the outer rim of a large, sturdy martini glass with a thin layer of chocolate syrup, then roll it in crushed graham crackers. Add the vodka, dark-chocolate liqueur and crème de cacao and top with the coffee. Garnish with the whipped cream, toasted marshmallow and chocolate shavings.

Goldfinger

One of five spiked-coffee drinks on this spy-themed restaurant's menu, Goldfinger is named for the 1964 James Bond film.

Zola • Washington, D.C.

- ½ ounce brandy
- ½ ounce Goldschläger
- 1½ tablespoons honey
- 6 ounces hot strong coffee
- 2 tablespoons unsweetened whipped cream and ground cinnamon

In a mug or heatproof glass, combine the brandy, Goldschläger and honey, then stir in the coffee. Top with the whipped cream and sprinkle with cinnamon.

The One Walnut

One Walnut • Cleveland

One Walnut prepares this after-dinner cocktail with Nocello, an Italian walnut liqueur.

Ice
1½ ounces coconut rum
1 ounce coffee liqueur
½ ounce walnut liqueur
1½ teaspoons half-and-half
1 spiced or candied walnut (optional)

Fill a cocktail shaker with ice. Add the rum, liqueurs and half-and-half and shake well. Strain into a chilled martini glass and garnish with the walnut, if using.

Grand-Fashioned

Employees Only • New York City

This rich spin on the old-fashioned replaces navel orange and bourbon with blood orange, fresh lime juice and Grand Marnier.

½ blood orange, cut into quarters
½ ounce fresh lime juice
3 dashes of Angostura bitters
1 teaspoon superfine sugar
2 ounces Grand Marnier
Ice

In a cocktail shaker, muddle the blood orange, lime juice, bitters and sugar. Add the Grand Marnier and enough ice to fill a rocks glass and shake well. Pour—do not strain—into a rocks glass.

Golden Dragon

Sushi Roku • Las Vegas

Navan, a vanilla-flavored Cognac liqueur recently launched by Grand Marnier, and orgeat, a milky syrup made with almonds and orange-flower or rose water, are both featured in this creamy but not heavy cocktail.

Ice
1½ ounces aged rum
1 ounce cream of coconut from a well-shaken can
1 ounce milk
¾ ounce orgeat syrup
¾ ounce Navan
1 ounce chilled club soda
Pinch of ground cinnamon

Fill a cocktail shaker with ice. Add all of the ingredients except the club soda and cinnamon, shake well and strain into an ice-filled red wine glass. Top with the club soda and sprinkle with the cinnamon.

Toasted Coconut

Crush • San Diego

A honeycombed wall made of PVC piping serves as a striking backdrop (and clever bottle storage) for this restaurant's blue-lit bar.

Ice
2 ounces coconut rum
2 ounces pineapple juice
½ ounce Frangelico
1 teaspoon toasted unsweetened coconut flakes

Fill a cocktail shaker with ice. Add the rum, pineapple juice and Frangelico and shake well. Strain into a chilled martini glass and garnish with the toasted coconut flakes.

Aspen Sugar Daddy

Range Restaurant • Aspen

This drink uses Amarula, a widely available South African liqueur flavored with the tart fruit of the marula tree and reminiscent of Irish cream liqueur.

Splash of pomegranate juice and sugar
Ice
1½ ounces vodka
½ ounce triple sec
½ ounce Amarula
½ ounce pomegranate juice
1½ teaspoons fresh lime juice

Moisten the outer rim of a chilled martini glass with the pomegranate juice and coat with sugar. Fill a cocktail shaker with ice. Add all of the remaining ingredients, shake well and strain into the martini glass.

You're a Pepper, Too

Luna Park • Los Angeles

Luna Park mixes this drink with Dublin Dr Pepper. Bottled in Dublin, Texas, at the country's oldest Dr Pepper plant, it's the only version still made with sugar instead of corn syrup.

Ice
2 ounces vanilla vodka
1½ ounces vanilla syrup
4 ounces Dr Pepper
3 Dr Pepper–flavored jelly beans (optional)

Fill a highball glass with ice. Add the vodka and vanilla syrup, top with the Dr Pepper and garnish with the jelly beans, if using.

RINGO STAR
Teikoku, Newtown Square, PA

Blueberry Tea

Vault Martini • Portland, OR

This local art-filled bar in the Pearl District is a popular stop on Portland's monthly First Thursday Artwalk.

- 1½ ounces Grand Marnier
- 1½ teaspoons amaretto
- 6 ounces hot tea, preferably orange pekoe
- 1 lemon wedge

In a large brandy snifter, swirl together the Grand Marnier and amaretto. Add the hot tea and top with a squeeze of lemon.

Ringo Star

Teikoku • Newtown Square, PA

The name of this unusual sake-and-cider toddy refers to the Japanese word for "apple," *ringo*. "It's definitely *not* an ode to the Beatles' drummer," says mixologist and general manager Umer Naim.

- 2 ounces dry sake
- 1½ ounces apple cider
- ½ ounce caramel sauce
- 1 cinnamon stick

In a saucepan, gently warm the sake, cider and caramel sauce. Stir well, pour into a martini glass and garnish with the cinnamon stick.

Lemontonia

Blue Gin • Washington, D.C.

Lemontonia is the work of Blue Gin's Ukrainian-born, London-trained mixologist Antonia Andrasi. The addition of lemon curd makes the cocktail particularly rich.

Ice
- 2 ounces limoncello
- 2 ounces lemon curd
- 1 ounce vodka
- 1 ounce fresh lemon juice
- 1 orange twist

Fill a cocktail shaker with ice. Add all of the ingredients except the orange twist and shake well. Strain into a large chilled martini glass and garnish with the twist.

Lemon Sorbet Martini

The Bosco • Ferndale, MI

Brothers Jeremy and Daniel Haberman named The Bosco for their middle school playground. "Should we need a fancier interpretation," says Daniel, noting the bar's tree-shaded courtyard, "*bosco* also means 'forest' in Italian."

Ice
- 1 ounce vodka
- 1 ounce limoncello
- 1½ teaspoons peach schnapps
- 1 ounce lemonade
- ½ teaspoon heavy cream
- 1 lemon wheel

Fill a cocktail shaker with ice. Add all of the ingredients except the lemon wheel and shake well. Strain into a chilled martini glass and garnish with the lemon wheel.

Rapa Nui

At Drift, a South Pacific–themed restaurant, bartenders garnish this enormous dessert cocktail with a crispy plantain chip.

Drift • Scottsdale

- 1½ ounces brandy
- ½ ounce coffee liqueur
- ½ ounce crème de cacao
- 1½ cups vanilla ice cream
- 1 small ripe banana
- 2 tablespoons unsweetened whipped cream, freshly ground cinnamon and 1 plantain chip (optional)

In a blender, combine the brandy, coffee liqueur, crème de cacao, ice cream and banana and blend well. Pour into a red wine glass and garnish with the whipped cream, a sprinkle of cinnamon and the plantain chip, if using.

Butter Pecan

This restaurant pays tribute to Poole's Luncheonette, a downtown Raleigh landmark that opened as a pie shop in 1942.

Poole's Diner • Raleigh

- 1 cup butter pecan ice cream
- 1 ounce bourbon
- ½ ounce chocolate syrup
- 1½ teaspoons milk
- Pinch of malt powder (optional)
- 3 candied pecans (optional)

In a blender, combine all of the ingredients except the candied pecans and blend well. Pour into a chilled highball glass and garnish with the pecans, if using.

SANGRIA ROSADA, P. 185
Chez Henri, Cambridge, MA

PITCHER DRINKS

Emerald Star

This lively bar occupies a former Wells Fargo bank. The owners kept the bulletproof teller windows and the main vault, where bartenders serve beer and Jägermeister shots on Saturday nights.

White Collar Crime • Raleigh

MAKES 8 DRINKS

- 8 ounces light rum
- 8 ounces mango nectar or juice
- 4 ounces Midori
- 3 ounces apricot brandy
- 3 ounces fresh lime juice

Ice

- 8 lime wedges and 8 maraschino cherry skewers

1. In a pitcher, combine the light rum, mango nectar, Midori, apricot brandy and lime juice and refrigerate until chilled, about 2 hours.

2. Fill a cocktail shaker with ice and add a quarter of the chilled mixture. Shake well and strain into 2 chilled martini glasses. Repeat three times with fresh ice and the remaining mixture. Garnish each drink with a lime wedge and a maraschino cherry skewer.

Hurricane

With seating for 500 and panoramic views of New Orleans, Club 360 is the country's largest revolving lounge.

Club 360 • New Orleans

MAKES 8 DRINKS

24 ounces pineapple juice
24 ounces fresh orange juice
8 ounces light rum
8 ounces grenadine
Ice
8 ounces dark rum, preferably Myers's
8 orange wheels and 8 maraschino cherries

In a large nonmetallic container, combine the juices, light rum and grenadine and refrigerate until chilled, at least 2 hours. Stir well and ladle into ice-filled pint glasses. Top each drink with 1 ounce of dark rum and garnish with an orange wheel and a cherry.

Bob Marley

This cavernous restaurant's Yow Bar is named for Yow Low, one of the original bartenders at San Francisco's Trader Vic's restaurant and the creator of the potent Bob Marley cocktail.

Le Passage • Chicago

MAKES 8 DRINKS

12 ounces fresh orange juice
6 ounces overproof rum
6 ounces dark crème de cacao
6 ounces orange curaçao
4 ounces sweet vermouth
1½ ounces fresh lime juice
1 ounce grenadine
Ice

In a pitcher, combine all of the ingredients except the ice. Refrigerate until chilled, about 2 hours. Stir well and serve in ice-filled red wine glasses.

COQUITO
Carmen the Restaurant,
Coral Gables, FL

Coquito

Carmen the Restaurant • Coral Gables, FL

Demand for the Coquito, a Latin take on eggnog, was so great that Carmen now serves the drink year-round, not just during the holidays.

MAKES ABOUT 2 DOZEN DRINKS

2¼ cups water
Thick strips of zest from 2 limes
25 cinnamon sticks
2⅓ cups sugar (1 pound)
One 14-ounce can unsweetened coconut milk
One 12-ounce can evaporated milk
16 ounces light rum
¼ cup pure vanilla extract
3 large egg yolks (optional)

1. In a medium saucepan, combine the water with the lime zest and 1 cinnamon stick and simmer over moderate heat for 15 minutes. Strain into a large heatproof bowl and refrigerate until chilled, at least 1 hour.

2. Whisk in the sugar, coconut milk, evaporated milk, light rum, vanilla and egg yolks, if using; whisk until the sugar is dissolved. Refrigerate the drink until chilled, about 2 hours. Stir well and ladle into small chilled martini or cordial glasses; garnish with the remaining cinnamon sticks.

RUM PUNCH
Alma, San Francisco

Rum Punch

This recipe is easy to multiply for crowds. To ensure that a large batch stays chilled without becoming watery, serve it in a punch bowl set in a larger bowl of crushed ice.

Alma • San Francisco

MAKES 8 DRINKS

80 mint leaves, torn or thinly sliced
8 ounces light rum
8 ounces aged rum
8 ounces fresh orange juice
8 ounces mango nectar or juice
4 ounces pineapple juice
Ice
8 pineapple wedges

In a pitcher, combine all of the ingredients except the ice and pineapple wedges and refrigerate until chilled, about 2 hours. Stir well and serve over ice in red wine glasses. Garnish each drink with a pineapple wedge.

Sugar Baby

The Sam Bar is located in the newly renovated Sam Houston Hotel, where a 1920s sign still advertises two-dollar lodgings.

The Sam Bar • Houston

MAKES 2 DOZEN DRINKS

1 pound fresh pineapple cubes
2 vanilla beans, split
2 cinnamon sticks, broken up
1 liter vodka
Ice
About 1½ liters chilled Sprite

In a large nonmetallic container, combine all of the ingredients except the ice and Sprite. Mash the pineapple and vanilla beans. Cover and refrigerate for 5 to 7 days. Strain the infused vodka into ice-filled highball glasses and top with the Sprite.

Red Square

The cocktails at this restaurant in the newly renovated Museum of Modern Art are inspired by art. This smooth, borscht-like drink honors the Russian suprematist Kazimir Malevich's 1915 painting *Black Square and Red Square,* which is in MoMA's permanent collection.

The Modern • New York City

MAKES 20 DRINKS

- 6 medium red beets, scrubbed
- Salt
- 1 quart plus ⅓ cup water
- 16 ounces red wine, preferably Pinot Noir
- ½ medium onion, sliced
- 1 tablespoon crushed red pepper
- 1 tablespoon whole black peppercorns
- 1 teaspoon fennel seeds
- 1 teaspoon cumin seeds
- 1 sprig each of rosemary, thyme, sage and basil
- Ice
- 11 ounces vodka

1. Preheat the oven to 375°. Place the beets on a sheet of foil, sprinkle with salt and add the ⅓ cup of water. Wrap the beets tightly, set the package on a baking sheet and roast until tender, about 2 hours. Carefully unwrap and let cool.

2. Peel and coarsely chop the beets. Transfer to a large pot and add all of the remaining ingredients except the ice and vodka. Cook over moderately high heat, stirring occasionally, until the liquid has reduced to 2 cups, about 30 minutes. Strain the beet juice through a fine sieve and refrigerate until chilled.

3. Fill a cocktail shaker with ice. Add 2¾ ounces of the vodka and 4 ounces of the spicy beet juice and shake well. Strain into 5 chilled cordial glasses. Repeat three more times, using fresh ice each time.

Hollow Hills

This bar is named for the conjoined daughters of Mario Guccio, a friend of the owners. *Salotto* is Italian for "lounge."

Mario's Double Daughter's Salotto • Denver

MAKES 8 DRINKS

12 ounces vodka
8 ounces Tuaca
8 ounces apricot juice or nectar
8 ounces apple juice
4 ounces pomegranate juice
Ice

In a pitcher, combine all of the ingredients except the ice and refrigerate until chilled, about 2 hours. Stir well and serve over ice in highball glasses.

The Sultan

Mie N Yu's decor borrows from Morocco, Tibet, Turkey and Italy and includes an English-style bar.

Mie N Yu • Washington, D.C.

MAKES 6 DRINKS

10 ounces vodka
6 ounces fresh orange juice
4 ounces fresh grapefruit juice
3 ounces triple sec
2 ounces Red Bull energy drink
8 ounces chilled club soda
8 orange twists

In a pitcher, combine all of the ingredients except the club soda and orange twists and refrigerate until chilled, about 2 hours. Stir well and pour into ice-filled red wine glasses. Top each drink with 1 ounce of club soda and garnish with an orange twist.

PACIFIC BREEZE
Pacific'O, Lahaina, Maui

Pacific Breeze

This blue-streaked, vodka-spiked lemonade is popular on Pacific'O's torch-lit patio, just steps from the beach.

Pacific'O • Lahaina, Maui

MAKES 8 DRINKS

8 ounces black currant vodka
32 ounces lemonade
Ice
1 ounce blue curaçao
8 lemon wheels and 8 mint sprigs

In a pitcher, combine the vodka and lemonade and refrigerate until thoroughly chilled, about 2 hours. Stir well and pour into ice-filled highball or red wine glasses. Top each drink with ¾ teaspoon of blue curaçao and garnish with a lemon wheel and a mint sprig.

Ruby Red

The owners considered leaving the bar unnamed but decided instead to combine its location (32nd Avenue) with a vague astrological reference (one of the owners is a Pisces).

Swimclub 32 • Denver

MAKES 8 DRINKS

16 ounces grapefruit vodka
8 ounces triple sec
20 ounces fresh red grapefruit juice
4 ounces fresh orange juice
Ice
16 ounces chilled club soda
8 orange wheels

In a pitcher, combine the vodka, triple sec and citrus juices and refrigerate until chilled, about 2 hours. Stir well and pour into large ice-filled rocks glasses. Top each drink with 2 ounces of club soda and garnish with an orange wheel.

Tea-tini

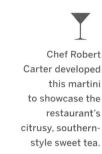

Chef Robert Carter developed this martini to showcase the restaurant's citrusy, southern-style sweet tea.

Peninsula Grill • Charleston

MAKES 8 DRINKS

16 ounces orange vodka
16 ounces Citrus Sweet Tea (below)
Ice
8 lemon wedges

In a large container, combine the vodka and Citrus Sweet Tea and refrigerate until chilled, at least 2 hours. Stir well. Half-fill a cocktail shaker with ice and add 8 ounces of the mixture. Shake well and strain into 2 chilled martini glasses. Repeat three more times, using fresh ice each time. Garnish each drink with a lemon wedge.

CITRUS SWEET TEA Steep 2 orange pekoe tea bags in 2 cups of boiling water for 5 minutes; discard the bags. Refrigerate the tea until cold, then stir in ½ cup of sugar, 2 tablespoons of fresh orange juice, 1 tablespoon of fresh lime juice and 1 tablespoon of fresh lemon juice. Stir until the sugar is dissolved. Refrigerate for up to 1 day. Makes 18 ounces of tea.

Chilango

The secret to this Mexican restaurant's award-winning spicy margarita is the sweet and smoky house-made chili powder that rims the glass.

El Chile Café y Cantina • Austin

MAKES 6 DRINKS

1 lime wedge
Chili powder
One 12-ounce can frozen limeade concentrate
12 ounces gold or reposado tequila
⅓ cup triple sec
4 cups ice
4 ounces fresh orange juice
4 ounces fresh lime juice
½ teaspoon Tabasco sauce

Moisten the outer rims of 6 margarita glasses with the lime wedge and coat lightly with chili powder. In a blender, combine the frozen limeade, tequila, triple sec and ice and blend well. Stir in the orange juice, lime juice and Tabasco sauce. Pour the drinks into the prepared margarita glasses and dust each one with chili powder.

CHINATOWN SLING
Nob Hill, Las Vegas

Chinatown Sling

This drink is based on the Singapore sling, created at Singapore's renowned Raffles Hotel in 1915.

Nob Hill • Las Vegas

MAKES 8 DRINKS

16 ounces pineapple juice
10 ounces gin
4 ounces triple sec
4 ounces Bénédictine
1 scant teaspoon Angostura bitters
Ice
2 ounces cherry liqueur, preferably Cherry Heering
8 pineapple spears and 8 maraschino cherries

In a pitcher, combine the pineapple juice, gin, triple sec, Bénédictine and bitters and refrigerate until chilled, about 2 hours. Stir well and pour into ice-filled rocks glasses. Top each drink with ¼ ounce of cherry liqueur and garnish with a pineapple spear and a maraschino cherry.

Starlight

Michael Mina • Las Vegas

The drinks here are based on famous San Francisco cocktails, like the signature recipe from Harry Denton's Starlight Room in the Sir Francis Drake Hotel.

MAKES 8 DRINKS

12 ounces Campari
8 ounces fresh orange juice
6 ounces triple sec
4 ounces fresh lemon juice
3 ounces Simple Syrup (P. 17)
2 ounces Cognac
Ice
16 ounces chilled club soda
8 lemon wheels and 8 lime wheels

In a pitcher, combine the Campari, fresh orange juice, triple sec, fresh lemon juice, Simple Syrup and Cognac. Refrigerate until chilled, about 2 hours. Stir the mixture well, then pour into ice-filled highball or red wine glasses. Top each drink with 2 ounces of chilled club soda and garnish with the lemon and lime wheels.

Midtown Sangria

Spice • Atlanta

"Cocktail engineer" Gina Word prepared her first batch of Midtown Sangria at the countercultural Burning Man festival in the Nevada desert. "I lived on that and hummus for a week," she says.

MAKES 8 DRINKS

1½ cups water
3 tablespoons orange-clover honey
¼ teaspoon ground cinnamon
One 750-ml bottle dry but fruity white wine, such as Sauvignon Blanc
12 ounces apple juice
8 orange wheels

In a glass bowl, combine the water, honey and ground cinnamon and microwave at high power for 40 seconds. Stir well, then pour into a large pitcher and add the white wine and apple juice. Refrigerate the sangria until chilled, at least 2 hours. Stir well and pour into ice-filled red wine glasses. Garnish each drink with an orange wheel.

THE PAYSAN
Poste, Washington, D.C.

Sangria Rosada

This rosé-based sangria reflects the restaurant's French and Latin influences.

Chez Henri • Cambridge, MA

MAKES 8 DRINKS

One 750-ml bottle dry rosé wine
4 ounces brandy
2 ounces maraschino liqueur
3 ounces guava nectar or juice
Ice
8 ounces chilled ginger ale
8 orange wheels and 8 maraschino cherries

In a pitcher, combine the wine, brandy, liqueur and guava nectar. Refrigerate until chilled, about 2 hours. Stir well and pour into ice-filled highball glasses. Top each drink with 1 ounce of ginger ale and garnish with an orange wheel and a cherry.

The Paysan

This Penn Quarter brasserie was formerly the mail-sorting room of the D.C. post office; diners use the same entrance that once accommodated horse-drawn mail carriages.

Poste • Washington, D.C.

MAKES 6 DRINKS

16 ounces fruity red wine, preferably Pinot Noir
8 ounces cranberry juice
4 ounces fresh orange juice
4 ounces Chambord
Ice
3 ounces chilled Sprite
Thinly sliced lemon, lime and orange zest

In a pitcher, combine the wine, juices and Chambord; refrigerate until chilled, about 2 hours. Stir well and pour into ice-filled white wine glasses. Top each drink with ½ ounce of Sprite and garnish with the zests.

VENTO FIZZ, P. 189
Vento, New York City

VIRGIN COCKTAILS

Tart Cherry Tonic

This restaurant and lounge occupies all three floors plus the roof of a century-old building that once housed a movie theater, a car dealership and a dental academy.

Tonic of Uptown • Minneapolis

Ice
- 5 ounces cherry juice
- 1½ ounces fresh lime juice
- 1½ ounces Simple Syrup (P. 17)
- 2 ounces chilled 7 UP
- 1 lime wedge

Fill a pint glass with ice. Add the cherry juice, lime juice and Simple Syrup and stir well. Top with the 7 UP, then squeeze the lime wedge over the drink and drop it in.

It's a Girl!

This tart pink cocktail was developed for expectant mothers. La Bourse also makes a boy version, with blueberries, white grape juice and lemon sorbet.

La Bourse • Philadelphia

MAKES 2 DRINKS

- 8 ounces fresh red grapefruit juice
- ½ cup fresh raspberries, plus 2 raspberries for garnish
- 4 ounces cranberry juice
- ½ cup crushed ice
- ¼ cup raspberry sorbet

In a blender, combine all of the ingredients except the raspberry garnish and blend well. Pour into 2 large chilled martini glasses and garnish each with a raspberry.

Vento Fizz

Vento • New York City

Originally a horse stable, this restaurant's downstairs lounge, Level V, was more recently a bondage-themed nightclub.

MAKES 6 DRINKS

Three 3.4-ounce bottles Sanbittèr soda
32 ounces fresh orange juice
One 8.5-ounce can peaches in heavy syrup, drained and finely diced
6 ounces chilled club soda

In a pitcher, combine the Sanbittèr soda, orange juice and peaches and refrigerate until chilled, at least 3 hours. Stir well, then spoon the peaches into 6 chilled Champagne flutes. Fill each flute almost completely with the Sanbittèr mixture and top with the club soda.

Horchata

SoHo Cantina • New York City

Chef Ricardo Hernandez makes this Mexican rice milk, a childhood favorite, from his mother's recipe.

MAKES 4 TO 6 DRINKS

2 cups water
½ cup white rice
½ cup evaporated milk
2 tablespoons sugar
¼ to ½ teaspoon ground cinnamon, plus more for garnish
Ice

Combine all of the ingredients except the ice in a glass jar, seal and let sit overnight. Puree in a blender until smooth, then strain and pour into ice-filled red wine glasses. Garnish each drink with a pinch of ground cinnamon.

POM-POM
Taj, New York City

Pom-Pom

Pom-Pom is a nonalcoholic version of "cocktail stylist" Jerri Banks's Pomander, made with silver tequila and Falernum, a Caribbean liqueur flavored with lime. Falernum is available online and in some liquor stores.

Taj • New York City

Ice
1 ounce pomegranate juice
½ ounce mango nectar or juice
½ ounce Clove Tea (below)
½ ounce fresh lime juice
1 ounce chilled club soda
1 orange wheel

Fill a cocktail shaker with ice. Add the pomegranate juice, mango nectar, Clove Tea and lime juice and shake well. Strain into a chilled martini glass, top with the club soda and garnish with the orange wheel.

CLOVE TEA Steep 1 tablespoon of whole cloves in 1 cup of boiling water for 5 minutes. Strain and refrigerate for up to 3 days. Makes 8 ounces of tea.

Raspberry Crush

Rathbun's also serves an alcoholic version of this drink using raspberry vodka in place of the club soda.

Rathbun's • Atlanta

3 raspberries
1 teaspoon sugar
4 ounces chilled, strong green tea
½ ounce fresh lime juice
Ice
2 ounces chilled club soda

In a cocktail shaker, muddle 2 of the raspberries with the sugar. Add the tea, lime juice and ice; shake well. Strain into a highball glass over ice, top with the soda and garnish with the remaining raspberry.

Zen High

Frisson • San Francisco

Mixologist Duggan McDonnell specializes in elaborate cocktails made with esoteric ingredients—like this tea-based drink flavored with wildflower honey and ginseng.

Ice
- **2 ounces chilled green tea**
- **½ teaspoon wildflower honey**
- **½ ounce fresh orange juice**
- **1½ teaspoons mango syrup**
- **1½ teaspoons Ginseng Syrup (below)**
- **1 lemon twist**

Fill a cocktail shaker with ice. Add all of the ingredients except the lemon twist and shake well. Strain into a chilled martini glass and garnish with the lemon twist.

GINSENG SYRUP Add 2 drops of Siberian ginseng to 4 ounces of Simple Syrup (P. 17).

Green Tea Soda

Saucebox • Portland, OR

Owner Joe Rogers found the name for his bar in Shakespeare's *The Taming of the Shrew,* where it refers to an unruly child.

Ice
- **1½ ounces Green Tea Syrup (below)**
- **8 ounces chilled club soda**

Fill a 15-ounce pint glass with ice. Add the Green Tea Syrup, top with the club soda and stir.

GREEN TEA SYRUP Steep 2 bags of green tea in 1 cup of boiling water for 5 minutes, then discard. Add 1 cup of sugar and stir until dissolved. Let cool, then refrigerate for up to 1 week. Makes 10 ounces of syrup.

Eli's Refresher

This bright-tasting drink was created for chef and co-owner Mitchell Rosenthal's five-year-old son, Eli.

Town Hall • San Francisco

Ice
3 ounces Fresh Mint Syrup (below)
3 ounces peach nectar or juice
2 ounces ginger beer
1½ ounces guava nectar or juice
½ ounce fresh lime juice
1½ teaspoons pineapple juice
1½ teaspoons apple juice
1 mint sprig

Fill a cocktail shaker with ice. Add all of the ingredients except the mint sprig and shake well. Strain into a chilled highball glass and garnish with the mint sprig.

FRESH MINT SYRUP Steep ¼ cup of packed bruised mint sprigs in ½ cup of very hot water for 10 minutes. Add 1 heaping teaspoon of sugar and muddle well. Strain and refrigerate for up to 1 week. Makes 4 ounces of syrup.

GINGER-MINT LEMONADE
Flatiron Lounge,
New York City

Irie Heights

Owner Donna Moodie named her restaurant in honor of her Jamaican mother, Marjorie. "Irie Heights" is a Jamaican expression that means "feeling great."

Marjorie • Seattle

Ice
2 ounces coconut water
1 ounce fresh lime juice
1 ounce Ginger Syrup (P. 145)
2 ounces chilled club soda
1 lime wedge

Fill a cocktail shaker with ice. Add the coconut water, lime juice and Ginger Syrup and shake well. Strain into a highball glass over ice. Top with the club soda and a squeeze of lime and stir well.

Ginger-Mint Lemonade

Flatiron Lounge's 30-foot mahogany bar was built in 1927 for the Manhattan Ballroom, a Frank Sinatra hangout.

Flatiron Lounge • New York City

10 mint leaves
1 ounce Simple Syrup (P. 17)
1 tablespoon finely grated, peeled fresh ginger
1½ ounces fresh lemon juice
3 tablespoons water
Ice
1 lemon wheel and 1 mint sprig

In a cocktail shaker, muddle the mint leaves with the Simple Syrup. Add the ginger, lemon juice, water and ice and shake well. Strain into a small highball glass over ice and garnish with the lemon wheel and mint sprig.

THE GUIDE

A coast-to-coast guide to some of the most exciting nightlife in America.

Here is a listing of the bars, restaurants and lounges that provided cocktails for this book (see the pages indicated below), plus other hot spots you should know about.

ASPEN

Jimmy's
P. 94
Tequila temple
205 S. Mill St.
970-925-6020

Matsuhisa Lounge
Sushi hangout
303 E. Main St.
970-544-6628

Range Restaurant
P. 161
Rocky Mountain menu
304 E. Hopkins Ave.
970-925-2402

ATLANTA AREA

Bar Joël
Stylish scene
3290 Northside Pkwy.
404-233-3500

Compound
P. 83
Sleek lounge with DJs
1008 Brady Ave.
404-872-4621

Inman Park Patio
P. 115
Neighborhood favorite
1029 Edgewood Ave. NE
404-659-5757

Luxe
Renovated mansion
89 Park Pl., downtown
404-389-0800

MidCity Cuisine
P. 45
New American brasserie
1545 Peachtree St.
404-888-8700

ONE. midtown kitchen
Cool warehouse space
559 Dutch Valley Rd.
404-892-4111

Rathbun's
P. 191
Clever southern menu
112 Krog St.
404-524-8280

Restaurant Eugene
Discreetly opulent hideaway
2277 Peachtree Rd.
404-355-0321

Sala
Tex-Mex mecca
1186 N. Highland Ave. NE
404-872-7203

Spice
P. 183
Miami Vice vibe, international menu
793 Juniper St.
404-875-4242

Sweet Devil Moon
Peruvian tapas lounge
350 Mead Rd.
Decatur
404-371-3999

TWO. urban licks
Blues and ribs joint
820 Ralph McGill Blvd.
404-522-4622

AUSTIN

Club de Ville
Musicians' haunt
900 Red River St.
512-457-0900

El Chile Café y Cantina
P. 179
Margarita central
1809 Manor Rd.
512-457-9900

Four Seasons Hotel
Urban cowboy hangout
98 San Jacinto Blvd.
512-478-4500

Saba Blue Water Cafe
P. 95
Aquatic-themed watering hole
208-D W. 4th St.
512-478-7222

219 West
P. 98
Music-lover's scene
219 W. 4th St.
512-474-2194

BALTIMORE

Good Love Bar
Dancing and DJs
2322 Boston St.
410-534-4588

Pazo
P. 36
Small plates, huge space
1425 Aliceanna St.
410-534-7296

Red Maple
Electronica and Asian tapas
930 N. Charles St.
410-547-0149

Spy Club
Kitschy lounge
15 E. Centre St.
410-685-4779

Tusk Lounge
P. 91
Upscale upstairs haven
924 N. Charles St.
410-547-8485

BOSTON AREA

B-Side Lounge
P. 85
Punk rock meets Rat Pack
92 Hampshire St.
Cambridge
617-354-0766

Chez Henri
P. 185
French-Cuban bistro
1 Shepard St.
Cambridge
617-354-8980

Cuchi Cuchi
P. 65
Belle Epoque throwback
795 Main St.
Cambridge
617-864-2929

Excelsior
P. 115
Contemporary American cuisine
The Heritage on the Garden
272 Boylston St.
617-426-7878

Grill 23 & Bar
P. 139
Sophisticated steak house
161 Berkeley St.
617-542-2255

Mantra
P. 47
French-Indian restaurant
52 Temple Pl.
617-542-0111

Mistral
P. 127
Provençal retreat
223 Columbus Ave.
617-867-9300

No. 9 Park
P. 83
French-Italian foodie favorite
9 Park St.
617-742-9991

Pho Republique
P. 46
Lantern-lit restaurant and lounge
1415 Washington St.
617-262-0005

Silvertone Bar & Grill
Subterranean retro refuge
69 Bromfield St.
617-338-7887

33 Restaurant & Lounge
Trendy Euro crowd
33 Stanhope St.
617-572-3311

Union Bar and Grille
P. 41
New American bastion
1357 Washington St.
617-423-0555

UpStairs on the Square
P. 112
Eccentric forties glam
91 Winthrop St.
Cambridge
617-864-1933

CHARLESTON AREA

High Cotton
P. 154
Hemingway vibe
199 E. Bay St.
843-724-3815

McCrady's
P. 112
Luxe low country
2 Unity Alley
843-577-0025

Pavilion Bar
P. 147
Panoramic views
Market Pavilion Hotel
225 E. Bay St.
843-723-0500

Peninsula Grill
P. 178
Historic elegance
112 N. Market St.
843-723-0700

Zinc Bistro & Bar
P. 42
Harborside hangout
28A Bridgeside Blvd.
Mount Pleasant
843-216-9330

CHICAGO

De Cero
P. 97
Modern Mexican
814 W. Randolph St.
312-455-8114

Elm Street Liquors
P. 23
Nouveau speakeasy
12 W. Elm St.
312-337-3200

Gibsons Steakhouse
Steak-and-martini club
1028 N. Rush St.
312-266-8999

Japonais
P. 29
Jet-set Japanese
600 W. Chicago Ave.
312-822-9600

Le Passage
P. 169
Velvet-rope hot spot
937 N. Rush St.
312-255-0022

Matchbox
P. 50
Small and swanky
770 N. Milwaukee Ave.
312-666-9292

Monsoon
P. 75
Indian-Asian menu
2813 N. Broadway
773-665-9463

N9NE
Modern steak house
440 W. Randolph St.
312-575-9900

Rockit Bar & Grill
Wild West meets rock and roll
22 W. Hubbard St.
312-645-6000

Silver Cloud
P. 158
Forties-style comfort zone
1700 N. Damen Ave.
773-489-6212

Sushi Samba Rio
P. 37
Japanese-Brazilian-Peruvian fusion
504 N. Wells
312-595-2300

Wave
Lakefront hotel lounge
W Chicago–Lakeshore
644 N. Lake Shore Dr.
312-943-9200

CLEVELAND

Century
P. 144
Martini and sushi bar
Ritz-Carlton Cleveland
1515 W. 3rd St.
216-902-5255

806 Wine & Martini Bar
Retro-glam haunt
806 Literary Rd.
216-696-4806

Fahrenheit
P. 84
Bustling modern American
2417 Professor Ave.
216-781-8858

One Walnut
P. 159
Art Deco den
1801 E. 9th St.
216-575-1111

2527
P. 116
Nightclub with live music
2527 W. 25th St.
216-771-2527

The Velvet Tango Room
P. 131
Soviet-style speakeasy
2095 Columbus Rd.
216-241-8869

DALLAS

Arcodoro & Pomodoro
P. 134
Grappa specialists
2708 Routh St.
214-871-1924

Dragonfly
P. 24
Luxe Med-Asian
Hotel ZaZa
2332 Leonard St.
214-550-9500

The Drálion
P. 127
Sultry Asian restaurant and lounge
3102 Oak Lawn Ave.
Ste. 110
214-219-6880

Ferré
P. 155
Tuscan restaurant
3699 McKinney Ave.
Ste. 106
214-522-3888

Moosh
P. 57
Sleek Japanese bar with DJs
2018 Greenville Ave.
214-824-7752

Nana
Posh hotel restaurant
Wyndham Anatole
2201 Stemmons Fwy.
214-761-7470

DENVER/BOULDER

The Cruise Room
Art Deco bar
Oxford Hotel
1600 17th St.
Denver
303-825-1107

Flow
P. 60
Velvet-rope hotel bar
Luna Hotel
1612 Wazee St.
Denver
303-572-3300

Forest Room 5
P. 125
Gallery space with live music
2532 15th St.
Denver
303-433-7001

Frasca
P. 89
Italian canteen
1738 Pearl St.
Boulder
303-442-6966

The Kitchen
Upscale eco-eatery
1039 Pearl St.
Boulder
303-544-5973

Mario's Double Daughter's Salotto
P. 175
Carnivalesque watering hole
1632 Market St.
Denver
303-623-3505

Mateo
Provençal bistro and bar
1837 Pearl St.
Boulder
303-443-7766

Mirepoix
P. 149
New American stronghold
JW Marriott Denver
at Cherry Creek
150 Clayton Lane
Denver
303-253-3000

My Brother's Bar
Cool burger spot
2376 15th St.
Denver
303-455-9991

Sputnik
P. 87
Kitschy bar and juke joint
7 S. Broadway
Denver
720-570-4503

Swimclub 32
P. 177
Asian-inspired tapas lounge
3628 W. 32nd Ave.
Denver
720-889-7946

Zengo
P. 31
Asian-Latin fusion
1610 Little Raven St.
Denver
720-904-0965

DETROIT AREA

Blue Martini
P. 33
Live music scene
201 Hamilton Row
Birmingham
248-258-3005

The Bosco
P. 164
Eclectic lounge
22930 Woodward Ave.
Ferndale
248-541-8818

Cinq
P. 147
Subterranean sanctuary
419 S. Main St.
Royal Oak
248-544-6250

Crave
P. 80
Minimalist pan-Asian
22075 Michigan Ave.
Dearborn
313-277-7283

Double Olive
Fifties- and sixties-inspired cocktail lounge
15130 Mack Ave.
Grosse Pointe Park
313-823-8892

Forté
American brasserie
201 S. Old Woodward Ave.
Birmingham
248-594-7300

FT. LAUDERDALE

Johnny V
P. 73
Floribbean restaurant
625 E. Las Olas Blvd.
954-761-7920

Trina
P. 84
Destination drinks menu
The Atlantic
601 N. Fort Lauderdale Beach Blvd.
954-567-8070

HAWAII

Alan Wong's Restaurant at King Street
Star chef stronghold
1857 S. King St., 3rd Fl.
Honolulu
808-949-2526

The Beach Bar
Waterside live-music bar
Moana Surfrider
2365 Kalakaua Ave.
Honolulu
808-922-3111

Diamond Head Grill
P. 27
Posh hotel restaurant and lounge
W Honolulu–Diamond Head
2885 Kalakaua Ave., 2nd Fl.
Honolulu
808-922-3734

House Without a Key
P. 72
Tree-shaded cocktail oasis
Halekulani
2199 Kalia Rd.
Honolulu
808-923-2311

Indigo
P. 43
Live jazz joint
1121 Nu'uanu Ave.
Honolulu
808-521-2900

Murphy's Bar & Grill
Old-school Irish pub
2 Merchant St.
Honolulu
808-531-0422

Pacific'O
P. 177
Oceanside dining
505 Front St.
Lahaina, Maui
808-661-8422

HOUSTON

Benjy's
P. 21
Asian-influenced restaurant and lounge
2424 Dunstan St.
713-522-7602

Bistro Moderne
Boutique-hotel restaurant and bar
Hotel Derek
2525 W. Loop South
713-961-3000

Cecil's Tavern
Casual neighborhood pub
600 W. Gray St.
713-527-9101

The Davenport
P. 142
Rat Pack–esque lounge
2115 Richmond Ave.
713-520-1140

Ibiza
Breezy Mediterranean
2450 Louisiana St.
Ste. 300
713-524-0004

The Mercury Room
Plush power scene
1008 Prairie St.
713-225-6372

The Sam Bar
P. 173
Cowboy-cool boutique-hotel bar
Sam Houston Hotel
1117 Prairie St.
877-348-8800

The Social
P. 25
Retro-chic DJ lounge
3730 Washington Ave.
713-426-5585

Under the Volcano
P. 73
Laid-back juke joint
2349 Bissonnet St.
713-526-5282

The Whiskey
P. 105
Candlelight meets rock and roll
Hotel Icon
220 Main St.
713-224-4266

LAS VEGAS

Boa Steakhouse
P. 26
Steak house with stunning views
Caesars Palace
3500 Las Vegas Blvd. South
702-733-7373

Bouchon
P. 143
Pewter-bar bistro
The Venetian
3355 Las Vegas Blvd. South
702-414-6200

Bradley Ogden
P. 99
Zen casino retreat
Caesars Palace
3570 Las Vegas Blvd. South
702-731-7410

Diego
P. 109
Modern Mexican
MGM Grand
3799 Las Vegas Blvd. South
702-891-3200

Fix
P. 81
Singles-scene extraordinaire
The Bellagio
3600 Las Vegas Blvd. South
702-693-8400

Ghostbar
Velvet-rope lounge
Palms Hotel & Casino
4321 W. Flamingo Rd.
702-942-7777

I-Bar
P. 104
Brazilian-themed casino bar
Rio All-Suite Hotel & Casino
3700 W. Flamingo Rd.
702-777-6869

Lure
Sleek new lounge scene
Wynn Las Vegas Country Club & Resort
3131 Las Vegas Blvd. South
702-770-7000

Michael Mina
P. 182
Seafood specialists
The Bellagio
3600 Las Vegas Blvd. South
702-693-7223

Nob Hill
P. 181
San Francisco homage
MGM Grand
3799 Las Vegas Blvd. South
702-891-7337

Shibuya
Sake stronghold
MGM Grand
3799 Las Vegas Blvd. South
702-891-3001

Sushi Roku
P. 160
Serene LA sushi bar outpost
Forum Shops
3500 Las Vegas Blvd. South
702-733-7373

Very Venice Bar
P. 21
Italianate resort lounge
The Venetian
3355 Las Vegas Blvd. South
702-732-0268

LOS ANGELES AREA

The Abbey
P. 157
Sprawling coffeehouse-nightclub
692 N. Robertson Blvd.
West Hollywood
310-289-8410

Bar Marmont
P. 80
Sultry nightspot
8171 W. Sunset Blvd.
323-650-0575

Blue on Blue
Swanky poolside restaurant and lounge
Avalon Hotel
9400 W. Olympic Blvd.
Beverly Hills
310-277-5221

The Dime
Scarlet-hued hideaway
442 N. Fairfax Ave.
323-651-4421

The Dresden Room
Hipster supper club
1760 N. Vermont Ave.
Hollywood
323-665-4294

El Carmen
P. 95
Kitschy tequila institution
8138 W. 3rd St.
323-852-1552

Falcon
P. 55
Prime patio dining
7213 Sunset Blvd.
Hollywood
323-850-5350

Grace
P. 49
Romantic New American
7360 Beverly Blvd.
323-934-4400

The Hungry Cat
P. 113
Fancy clam shack
1535 N. Vine St.
Hollywood
323-462-2155

Koi Restaurant
Celebrity-friendly sushi spot
730 N. La Cienega Blvd.
310-659-9449

Lucques
P. 91
California-French
8474 Melrose Ave.
323-655-6277

Luna Park
P. 161
Whimsical comfort-food hangout
672 S. La Brea
323-934-2110

Maple Drive
Sleek movie-mogul favorite
345 N. Maple Dr.
Beverly Hills
310-274-9800

Musso & Frank's Grill
Landmark steak house
6667 Hollywood Blvd.
Hollywood
323-467-7788

Tangerine
Retro steak and seafood
8788 W. Sunset Blvd.
West Hollywood
310-360-0274

Voda
Vodka specialists
1449 2nd St.
Santa Monica
310-394-9774

LOUISVILLE

Avalon
P. 121
Bustling New American
1314 Bardstown Rd.
502-454-5336

Limestone
P. 120
New Southern restaurant
10001 Forest Green Blvd.
502-426-7477

The Oakroom
P. 157
Clubby turn-of-the-century restaurant
The Seelbach Hilton Louisville
500 S. 4th St.
502-807-3463

Park Place on Main
P. 116
Historic chophouse
401 E. Main St.
502-515-0172

Red Lounge
Boisterous industrial-chic bar
2106 Frankfort Ave.
502-896-6116

MEMPHIS

Automatic Slim's Tonga Club
P. 71
City-slicker juke joint
83 S. Second St.
901-525-7948

Beauty Shop
P. 131
Forties hair salon–turned–dining room
966 S. Cooper St.
901-272-7111

The Corner Bar
P. 81
Grand old-school bar
The Peabody
149 Union Ave.
901-529-4000

Grill 83
Oversized martini maker
83 Madison Ave.
901-333-1224

MIAMI AREA

Bahía
P. 47
Poolside hot spot with live Cuban music
Four Seasons Hotel Miami
1435 Brickell Ave.
305-358-3535

Carmen the Restaurant
P. 171
Modern Latino drinking and dining
David Williams Hotel
700 Biltmore Way
Coral Gables
305-913-1944

The District
Artists' favorite
35 NE 40th St.
305-576-7242

Martini Bar
PP. 53, 60
Art Deco hotel bar
Raleigh Hotel
1775 Collins Ave.
Miami Beach
305-534-6300

M-Bar
Martini haven
Mandarin Oriental, Miami
500 Brickell Key Dr.
305-913-8288

Prime One Twelve
Cool, kitschy steak house
The Browns Hotel
112 Ocean Dr.
Miami Beach
305-532-8112

Rumi
Mod-opulent restaurant and lounge
330 Lincoln Rd.
Miami Beach
305-672-4353

Sky Bar
P. 39
Lantern-lit indoor-outdoor lounge
The Shore Club
1901 Collins Ave.
Miami Beach
305-695-3100

Sushi Samba Dromo
P. 107
Melon-hued mod Asian-Latin
600 Lincoln Rd.
Miami Beach
305-673-5337

Talula
New American restaurant and bar
210 23rd St.
Miami Beach
305-672-0778

Tantra
Aphrodisiac vibe
1445 Pennsylvania Ave.
Miami Beach
305-672-4765

Touch
Velvet-rope restaurant with a carnival theme
910 Lincoln Rd.
Miami Beach
305-532-8003

MINNEAPOLIS AREA

Chino Latino
P. 103
Raucous party scene
2916 Hennepin Ave. South
612-824-7878

Cosmos
P. 119
Cool hotel restaurant and lounge
Le Meridien
601 1st Ave. North
612-677-1100

JP American Bistro
P. 63
Neighborhood standout
2937 Lyndale Ave. South
612-824-9300

Louis XIII
P. 25
Opulent salon
2670 Southdale Ctr.
Edina
952-746-4938

Red
Caviar den
821 Marquette Ave. South
612-436-8888

Tonic of Uptown
P. 188
Sprawling social scene
1400 W. Lake St.
612-824-8898

NEW ORLEANS

Cobalt
P. 148
Blue-themed boutique-hotel bar
Hotel Monaco New Orleans
333 Saint Charles Ave.
504-565-5595

d.b.a.
P. 42
Beer and whiskey bastion
618 Frenchmen St.
504-942-3731

Herbsaint
P. 151
Jazz club vibe
701 Saint Charles Ave.
504-524-4114

The Library Lounge
P. 124
Old-school elegance
Ritz-Carlton New Orleans
921 Canal St.
504-524-1331

Lilette
P. 120
Airy antiques-district spot
3637 Magazine St.
504-895-1636

Loa
P. 55
Cool candelit space
International House
221 Camp St.
504-553-9550

St. Joe's Bar
P. 61
Boisterous dive
5535 Magazine St.
504-899-3744

Club 360
P. 169
Revolving lounge
2 Canal St.
504-595-8900

NEW YORK CITY AREA

Angel's Share
Asian speakeasy
8 Stuyvesant St.
212-777-5415

Balthazar
P. 27
Glamorous SoHo brasserie
80 Spring St.
212-965-1785

Bar Masa
P. 30
Sushi sanctuary
10 Columbus Circle
212-823-9800

Bemelmans Bar
P. 130
Posh piano bar
The Carlyle
35 E. 76th St.
212-744-1600

Café Gray
French-fusion brasserie
10 Columbus Circle
212-823-6338

Employees Only
P. 159
Bartender-owned supper club
510 Hudson St.
212-242-3021

5 Ninth
PP. 75, 139
Mixologist's destination
5 9th Ave.
212-929-9460

Flatiron Lounge
PP. 76, 195
Art Deco chic
37 W. 19th St.
212-727-7741

Hearth
P. 151
New American restaurant
403 E. 12th St.
646-602-1300

Kittichai
P. 24
Glamorous Thai
60 Thompson St.
212-219-2000

Little Branch
P. 130
Speakeasy and oyster bar
22 7th Ave. South

Little Giant
P. 135
Dollhouse-sized dining room
85 Orchard St.
212-226-5047

Mas
Farmhouse-chic restaurant
39 Downing St.
212-255-1790

Matsuri
P. 29
Cavernous sake den
369 W. 16th St.
212-243-6400

The Modern
P. 174
Sleek museum restaurant
Museum of Modern Art
9 W. 53rd St.
212-333-1220

The Odeon
P. 36
Old-school brasserie
145 W. Broadway
212-233-0507

Pace
PP. 88, 133
Sprawling Italian
121 Hudson St.
212-965-9500

Pegu Club
PP. 89, 138
Cocktail connoisseur's haunt
77 W. Houston St., 2nd Fl.
212-473-7348

Porcupine
P. 68
Snug bistro, classic drinks
20 Prince St.
212-966-8886

Schiller's Liquor Bar
P. 109
People-watching café
131 Rivington St.
212-260-4555

Silverleaf Tavern
P. 76
Clubby hotel bar
43 E. 38th St.
212-973-2550

SoHo Cantina
P. 189
Bustling taqueria
199 Prince St.
212-598-0303

Star Lounge
P. 121
Old-school hotel bar
Ritz-Carlton New York, Central Park
50 Central Park South
212-308-9100

Tabla
P. 155
Creative Indian-American
11 Madison Ave.
212-889-0667

Taj
PP. 125, 191
Indian-spiced lounge
48 W. 21st St.
212-620-3033

Tempo
P. 85
Mod Mediterranean
256 5th Ave.
Brooklyn
718-636-2020

Vento
P. 189
Trendy trattoria
675 Hudson St.
212-699-2400

WD-50
P. 101
Futuristic food mecca
50 Clinton St.
212-477-2900

PHILADELPHIA AREA

Buddakan
P. 138
Enormous Asian restaurant and lounge
325 Chestnut St.
215-574-9440

Cibucán
P. 99
Modern pan-Latin
2025 Sansom St.
215-231-9895

Continental Midtown
Penthouse patio bar
1801 Chestnut St.
215-567-1800

Cuba Libre
P. 69
Old Havana aura
10 S. 2nd St.
215-627-0666

El Vez
Whimsical Mexican
121 S. 13th St.
215-928-9800

Fork
P. 38
Velvet-draped bistro
306 Market St.
215-625-9425

La Bourse
P. 188
Hotel-lobby lounge with live piano
Sofitel Philadelphia
120 S. 17th St.
215-569-8300

Pod
Space-age Asian-fusion
3636 Sansom St.
215-387-1803

Tangerine
P. 43
Candlelit Moroccan
232 Market St.
215-627-5116

Teikoku
P. 163
Family-style Thai-Japanese
5492 W. Chester Pike
Newtown Square
610-644-8270

Twenty Manning
P. 20
Stylish industrial space
261 S. 20th St.
215-731-0900

Washington Square
P. 62
Parkside bistro
210 W. Washington Sq.
215-592-7787

PORTLAND, OR

Bluehour
P. 67
Modern Mediterranean
250 NW 13th Ave.
503-226-3394

Brazen Bean
P. 117
Victorian house–turned–lounge
2075 NW Glisan St.
503-294-0636

820
P. 69
Cavernous lantern-lit space
820 N. Russell St.
503-460-0820

Harrison
P. 119
Cigar-friendly restaurant and lounge
Fox Tower
838 SW Park Ave.
503-299-6161

Huber's
P. 154
Local legend
411 SW 3rd Ave.
503-228-5686

Paley's Place
P. 137
Market-driven bistro
1204 NW 21st St.
503-243-2403

Saucebox
P. 192
Creative Asian-inspired food and cocktails
214 SW Broadway
503-241-3393

Vault Martini
P. 163
Living-room vibe
226 NW 12th Ave.
503-224-4909

PROVIDENCE

CAV
P. 26
Antiques-filled fusion restaurant
14 Imperial Pl.
401-751-9164

Costantino's Ristorante
Family-run classic Italian
265 Atwells Ave.
401-528-1100

Lot 401
Asian-fusion restaurant and lounge
44 Hospital St.
401-490-3980

Mediterraneo
P. 134
Alfresco Italian
134 Atwells Ave.
401-331-7760

Moda
P. 45
Modern Mediterranean
525 S. Water St.
401-331-2288

Restaurant Oak
Comfort-food zone
959 Hope St.
401-273-7275

RALEIGH/
CHAPEL HILL AREA

Elaine's on Franklin
P. 97
Sophisticated southern
454 W. Franklin St.
Chapel Hill
919-960-2770

Enoteca Vin
P. 87
Sleek wine bar
410 Glenwood Ave.
Ste. 350
Raleigh
919-834-3070

Five Star Restaurant
Nouvelle Chinese hot spot
511 W. Hargett St.
Raleigh
919-833-3311

Havana Deluxe
Cigar-friendly club
437 Glenwood Ave.
Raleigh
919-831-0991

Lantern
P. 49
Romantic lantern-lit restaurant and bar
423 W. Franklin St.
Chapel Hill
919-969-8846

Orange County Social Club
Unpretentious local lounge
108 E. Main St.
Carrboro
919-933-0669

Poole's Diner
P. 165
Fifties lunch counter–turned–stylish diner and martini bar
426 S. McDowell St.
Raleigh
919-832-4477

Talullas
Cozy Turkish mezze joint
456 W. Franklin St.
Chapel Hill
919-933-1177

White Collar Crime
P. 168
Bar in a renovated bank
319 W. Davie St.
Raleigh
919-828-0055

ST. LOUIS

Absolutli Goosed
Upscale martini lounge
3196 S. Grand Blvd.
314-772-0400

Barcelona
Colorful Spanish tapas
34 N. Central Ave.
Clayton
314-863-9909

Café Eau
Swanky snacks in a restored Jazz Age hotel
Chase Park Plaza Hotel
212 N. Kingshighway Blvd.
314-454-9000

Delmar Restaurant & Lounge
P. 144
Retro jazz club
6235 Delmar Blvd.
314-725-6565

Fox & Hounds Tavern
P. 50
English country–style pub
6300 Clayton Rd.
314-647-7300

Mirasol
P. 61
Splashy Nuevo Latino newcomer
6144 Delmar Blvd.
314-721-6909

Modesto
P. 148
Hip tapas lounge
5257 Shaw Ave.
314-772-8272

Pin-Up Bowl
P. 123
Quirky bowling alley and martini lounge
6191 Delmar Blvd.
314-727-5555

Zoë Pan-Asian Café
P. 143
Stylishly spare pan-Asian
4753 McPherson Ave.
314-361-0013

SAN DIEGO AREA

Air Conditioned
Local hangout with DJs
4673 30th St.
619-501-9831

Crush
P. 160
Clubby blue-lit bar scene
530 University Ave.
619-291-1717

Parallel 33
P. 63
International menu
741 W. Washington St.
619-260-0033

Region
P. 20
Farmhouse-esque restaurant
3671 5th Ave.
619-299-6499

Roppongi
P. 23
Asian-noir space
875 Prospect St.
La Jolla
858-551-5252

Turf Supper Club
P. 37
Old-school chophouse
1116 25th St.
619-234-6363

SAN FRANCISCO AREA

Alma
P. 173
Sultry Nuevo Latino
1101 Valencia St.
415-401-8959

Bambuddha Lounge
P. 145
Hip Asian-inspired hotel lounge
Phoenix Hotel
601 Eddy St.
415-885-5088

Baraka
P. 33
Mediterranean tapas with a view
288 Connecticut St.
415-255-0387

Bix
Forties-style restaurant and bar
56 Gold St.
415-433-6300

César
P. 137
Sherry stronghold
1515 Shattuck Ave.
Berkeley
510-883-0222

Circolo
P. 88
Peruvian-inspired restaurant and lounge with DJs
500 Florida St.
415-553-8560

Cortez
P. 104
Whimsical boutique-hotel restaurant
Hotel Adagio
550 Geary St.
415-292-6360

Enrico's Sidewalk Cafe
P. 77
Old-school cocktail spot
504 Broadway
415-982-6223

Frisson
P. 192
Ultramodern menu
244 Jackson St.
415-956-3004

Harry Denton's Starlight Room
Legendary rooftop hotel bar
450 Powell St.
415-395-8595

Jade Bar
P. 41
Tri-level lounge
650 Gough St.
415-869-1900

Levende Lounge
P. 30
Gallery space and lounge
1710 Mission St.
415-864-5585

Nizza La Bella
P. 142
Cozy Italian-inflected bistro
825 San Pablo Ave.
Albany
510-526-2552

RoHan Lounge
P. 57
Korean soju specialists
3809 Geary Blvd.
415-221-5095

The Slanted Door
P. 71
Vietnamese restaurant with a star chef
584 Valencia St.
415-861-8032

Tallula
P. 31
Seductive Indian-French
4230 18th St.
415-437-6722

Tartare
Relaxed red-toned restaurant
550 Washington St.
415-434-3100

Tommy's Mexican Restaurant
P. 94
Margarita ambassadors
5929 Geary Blvd.
415-387-4747

Town Hall
P. 193
Charming New England–style restaurant
342 Howard St.
415-908-3900

Tunnel Top
Intimate hipster bar and club
601 Bush St.
415-986-8900

SANTA FE

Dragon Room
Spirited bar popular with locals
406 Old Santa Fe Trail
505-983-7712

El Farol
P. 106
Tapas traditionalists
808 Canyon Rd.
505-983-9912

Santacafé
P. 46
Asian- and Southwestern-inflected restaurant
231 Washington Ave.
505-984-1788

Staab House
P. 105
Victorian relic–turned–restaurant and cocktail lounge
La Posada de Santa Fe Resort & Spa
330 E. Palace Ave.
505-954-9670

Swig
P. 106
Hip retro-themed club
135 W. Palace Ave., 3rd Fl.
505-955-0400

SCOTTSDALE

AZ 88
Modern American
7353 E. Scottsdale Mall
480-994-5576

Cowboy Ciao
P. 123
Quirky Italian-Southwestern
7133 E. Stetson Dr.
480-946-3111

Crown Room
Swanky cocktail lounge
7419 E. Indian Plaza
480-423-0017

Drift
P. 165
Torch-lit tiki lounge
4341 N. 75th St.
480-949-8454

Fiamma Trattoria
P. 72
Sleek Italian
James Hotel
7353 E. Indian School Rd.
480-308-1111

Roaring Fork
P. 103
Rugged ranch decor
4800 N. Scottsdale Rd.
480-947-0795

Sea Saw
Serene Asian retreat
7133 E. Stetson Dr.
480-481-9463

Six
Intimate velvet-lined lounge
7316 E. Stetson Dr.
480-663-6620

SEATTLE AREA

Brasa
PP. 53, 135
Romantic Mediterranean
2107 3rd Ave.
206-728-4220

Campagne
Provençal mainstay
86 Pine St.
206-728-2800

Chapel
P. 56
Mortuary–turned–minimalist cocktail lounge
1600 Melrose Ave.
206-447-4180

Jäger
PP. 39, 65
Hip Euro tavern
148 Lake St. South
Kirkland
425-803-3310

Marjorie
P. 195
Funky multicultural bistro
2331 2nd Ave.
206-441-9842

Mona's
P. 68
Latin drinks and live jazz
6421 Latona Ave. NE
206-526-1188

The Terrace
P. 145
Old-school hotel bar
Fairmont Olympic Hotel
411 University St.
206-621-1700

Thaiku
Antiques-filled Thai
5410 Ballard Ave. NW
206-706-7807

Waterfront Seafood Grill
Seafood standout with amazing harbor views
2801 Alaskan Way
206-956-9171

Zig Zag Café
PP. 101, 124
Pike Place Market watering hole
1501 Western Ave.
Ste. 202
206-625-1146

WASHINGTON, D.C., AREA

Blue Gin
P. 164
Dance club with noted mixologist
1206 Wisconsin Ave. NW
202-965-5555

Ceiba
P. 77
Modern Latin style
701 14th St. NW
202-393-3983

CityZen
P. 117
New American newcomer
Mandarin Oriental,
Washington D.C.
1330 Maryland Ave. SW
202-787-6868

Degrees
P. 67
See-and-be-seen lounge
The Ritz-Carlton
Georgetown
3100 South St. NW
202-912-4100

Le Paradou
Elegant French
678 Indiana Ave. NW
202-347-6780

Mie N Yu
P. 175
Eclectic Georgetown hangout
3125 M St. NW
202-333-6122

Oyamel
Mexican small plates
2250B Crystal Dr.
Arlington, VA
703-413-2288

Poste
P. 185
Modern American brasserie
Hotel Monaco
555 8th St. NW
202-783-6060

Restaurant Eve
P. 51
Seasonal Old Town dining
110 S. Pitt St.
Alexandria, VA
703-706-0450

Round Robin Bar
P. 113
Classic hotel bar
Willard InterContinental
Washington
1401 Pennsylvania Ave. NW
202-637-744

Zaytinya
P. 149
Mezze specialists
701 9th St. NW
202-638-0800

Zola
PP. 133, 158
Spy-themed American restaurant
800 F St. NW
202-654-0999

Glassware Sources

CHAMPAGNE, SAKE & WINE

P. 18 "Onda" long drink glass by Covo from Interiology, 212-226-4707 or interiology-ny.com

P. 22 "Vienna" Champagne glass from Moss, 866-888-6677 or mossonline.com

P. 28 "Random Cut" martini glass from Calvin Klein, 800-294-7978; **Cocktail pick with amethyst** by Ryan Kundrat, 203-241-9676 or ryankundrat.com

P. 32 "Eliche" wine glass from Salviati, 212-725-4361 or salviati.com

VODKA

P. 34 "Classic" cocktail glass from Tiffany & Co., 800-843-3269 or tiffany.com

P. 40 "Sullivan" martini glass from Williams-Sonoma, 877-812-6235 or williams-sonoma.com

P. 44 "Polka Dot" martini glass by Artland, 800-663-8810 or cooking.com

P. 52 "Diamanti" small martini glass from Salviati, 212-725-4361 or salviati.com

P. 54 "Line Series" tumbler from Lazy Susan, 212-685-0181 or lazysusanusa.com

RUM

P. 58 "Century" martini glass (left) from Steuben, 800-783-8236 or steuben.com; **"1953" cocktail glass** (right) from Steuben, 800-783-8236 or steuben.com

P. 64 "Silhouette Line" martini glass by Ken Benson from Lazy Susan, 212-685-0181 or lazysusanusa.com

P. 66 "Tuscany Classics" Champagne saucer from Lenox, 800-223-4311 or lenox.com; **"Beehive" cocktail shaker** by Vollrath, 800-624-2051 or vollrath.com

P. 70 "Lucie" martini glass from Moser, 866-240-5115 or moserusa.com

P. 74 "Game" martini glass from Asprey, 800-883-2777 or asprey.com

GIN

P. 78 "Retro" martini glass from Pottery Barn, 888-779-5176 or potterybarn.com

P. 82 "Intermezzo" tumbler by Erika Lagerbielke from Orrefors, 856-768-5400 or orrefors.com

P. 86 "Vogue" martini glass from Crate and Barrel, 800-967-6696 or crateandbarrel.com

P. 90 "Portofino" martini glass from Salviati, 212-725-4361 or salviati.com

TEQUILA

P. 92 "Fino" universal glass by Dibbern from Lekker, 877-753-5537 or lekkerhome.com; **"3000" tongs** by Adam D. Tihany from Christofle, 877-728-4556

P. 96 "Grand Traditional" Champagne cup from Moss, 866-888-6677 or mossonline.com

P. 100 "#0604" 5-oz stem glass from Matsu, 617-266-9707 or matsuboston.com

P. 102 "Modern Graphic" highball glasses from Vera Wang, 800-839-8372 or verawang.com

P. 108 "Tapio" cocktail glass from Iittala, 856-910-1873

WHISKEY

P. 111 "Bourgueil" Champagne coupe (right) from Lalique, 212-355-6550

P. 114 "Patrician Service" Champagne cup by Josef Hoffman from Neue Galerie, 212-628-6200 or neuegalerie.org; **"Him" sterling silver martini pick** by Janet Torelli from Henry & Lulu, henryandlulu.com

P. 118 "Acqua" water tumbler from Alessi, 877-253-7749 or alessi.com

P. 122 "Finial" sterling silver olive pick from Asprey, 800-883-2777 or asprey.com

P. 126 "Evening" martini glass from Steuben, 800-783-8236 or steuben.com

BRANDY

P. 128 "Tuscany Classics" martini glass (left) from Lenox, 800-223-4311 or lenox.com; **"Balans" martini glass** (right) by Jan Johansson from Orrefors, 856-768-5400 or orrefors.com

P. 132 "Stiletto" wine glass from Vera Wang, 800-839-8372 or verawang.com

P. 136 "Fusion Ice" martini glass from Royal Doulton, 800-682-4462 or royaldoulton.com

LIQUEUR & VERMOUTH

P. 140 "1953" highball glass from Steuben, 800-783-8236 or steuben.com

P. 150 "Murano" water glass from Moss, 866-888-6677 or mossonline.com

DESSERT DRINKS

P. 152 "Vino Grande" cordial saucer (right) from WMF, 800-999-6347 or wmf-usa.com

P. 156 "Silhouette Line" highball glass by Ken Benson from Lazy Susan, 212-685-0181 or lazysusanusa.com

P. 162 "Symmetry" martini glass from Royal Doulton, 800-682-4462 or royaldoulton.com

PITCHER DRINKS

P. 166 "Capri" pitcher by Covo from Lekker, 877-753-5537 or lekkerhome.com; **"Havana" highball glass** from Asprey, 800-883-2777 or asprey.com

P. 170 "Mami" martini glass from Alessi, 877-253-7749 or alessi.com

P. 172 "Rondo" wine glass by Covo from Interiology, 212-226-4707 or interiology-ny.com

P. 180 "Mami" whiskey tumbler from Alessi, 877-253-7749 or alessi.com

P. 184 "Parker" wine glass from Calvin Klein, 800-294-7978

VIRGIN COCKTAILS

P. 186 "Tortoise" Champagne flute by Ted Muehling from Steuben, 800-783-8236 or steuben.com

P. 190 "Atalante" martini glass from Christofle, 877-728-4556 or christofle.com

P. 194 "Omni" glass from Saint-Louis Cristal, 800-238-5522

Drinks Index

GIN

LIQUEUR & VERMOUTH

PITCHER DRINKS

RUM

TEQUILA

VIRGIN COCKTAILS

VODKA

FOOD&WINE
BOOKS

More books from FOOD & WINE

Best of the Best
The best recipes from the 25 best cookbooks of the year.

Annual Cookbook 2005
An entire year of recipes.

Wine Guide 2005
The most up-to-date guide with more than 1,000 recommendations.

Available wherever books are sold, or call 1-800-284-4145 or log on to foodandwine.com.

FOOD&WINE